Praise for
The Power Manual

We need to get comfortable talking about and wielding power.
In this book, Cyndi Suarez does a great job of sharing theories about
power — academic, literary, and spiritual. There are also several unique
practical games to build people's capacity to understand and
leverage power, which I'm looking forward to trying out.

— Susan Misra, Co-Director, Management Assistance Group

Think you know all about power? Think again! Drawing from a wide range
of disciplines, Suarez gives practical guidance for cultivating individual
consciousness and building social power. She reminds us that "the state
of being of the social change agent is the most powerful force for change.
We can fight for freedom, or we can enact freedom."

— Cynthia Silva Parker, Senior Associate, Interaction Institute for Social Change

Cyndi Suarez has written a book for our time. The social movements of our
day have a conflicted relationship with power, endlessly deconstructing its
evils while actively yearning for it. We forget that in any conflict the
tendency is to become the mirror image of your opponent. There is great
confusion between the struggle for power and the quest of liberation.
Cyndi has written a comprehensive operations manual for living into the
tension of these distinctions and quite literally enacting our way to freedom.

— Gibran Rivera, Master Facilitator

Most discussions of power explore the intellectual, political and economic
dynamics that generate imbalances in our society. Perhaps that's why power
can seem so immutable: Our efforts to think or transact our way into a
social reordering seem to result in little more than incremental change.
In her book, *The Power Manual*, Cyndi Suarez brilliantly illuminates
what's missing. To exercise and understand power is an embodied,
creative, spiritual and at times even playful act.

— Deborah Frieze, Author, *Walk Out Walk On* and
Founding President, Boston Impact Initiative

This book is masterful. In *The Power Manual*, Cyndi Suarez refuses to accept the silos by which we organize our thinking and fields of knowledge. The result is an examination of power that honors the fullness of who we are as individual human beings and as social creatures. Moving across the political, spiritual, psychological, and gender self, she helps us understand power across our lived experience. *The Power Manual* is the handbook every person who considers themselves working to bring about a more just and compassionate world should read and carry with them throughout their journey.

— Ceasar McDowell, Professor of the Practice of Civic Design,
Massachusetts Institute of Technology (MIT)

Cyndi Suarez draws insights from a diverse array of intellectual and spiritual traditions and her own experience as a social change practitioner to show that the power for social change is already within us. But we must exercise it in a way that shifts from a dominating power over to a liberating power with. *The Power Manual* is an accessible yet deep exploration into the complexity of power, as well as guide to group exercises for unleashing our collective power.

— Penn Loh, Senior Lecturer and Director of Community Practice,
Tufts Department of Urban and Environmental Policy and Practice

The Power Manual

HOW TO MASTER
COMPLEX POWER DYNAMICS

Cyndi Suarez

new society
PUBLISHERS

Cover design by Diane McIntosh.
Illustration © iStock

Printed in Canada. Second printing January 2022.

Inquiries regarding requests to reprint all or part of *The Power Manual* should be addressed to New Society Publishers at the address below. To order directly from the publishers, please call toll-free (North America) 1-800-567-6772, or order online at www.newsociety.com

Any other inquiries can be directed by mail to:
New Society Publishers
P.O. Box 189, Gabriola Island, BC V0R 1X0, Canada
(250) 247-9737

LIBRARY AND ARCHIVES CANADA CATALOGUING IN PUBLICATION

Suarez, Cyndi, 1971-, author
   The power manual : how to master complex power dynamics / Cyndi Suarez.

Includes bibliographical references and index.
Issued in print and electronic formats.
ISBN 978-0-86571-881-4 (softcover).--ISBN 978-1-55092-674-3 (PDF).--ISBN 978-1-77142-269-7 (EPUB)

   1. Power (Social sciences). I. Title.

HN49.P6S83 2018   303.3   C2018-901506-3
                                C2018-901507-1

Funded by the
Government
of Canada

Financé par le
gouvernement
du Canada

Canada

New Society Publishers' mission is to publish books that contribute in fundamental ways to building an ecologically sustainable and just society, and to do so with the least possible impact on the environment, in a manner that models this vision.

MIX
Paper from
responsible sources
FSC
www.fsc.org
FSC® C016245

Certified
B
Corporation

new society
PUBLISHERS

Contents

Introduction
Why I Wrote This Book

I 've been wanting to write this book since I was a teenager. That's when I started reading feminist, political, and metaphysical theory. In my life, and in my mind, I was exploring the power that structures society and that social-change agents work to shift, and the power at the root of the soul, of one's manifestation in this life.

I grew up in Roxbury, Boston's historic black neighborhood. As a teenager, I understood that my neighborhood was marginal in the city of Boston. I wanted to understand how this subordinate social positioning was created and maintained. In a sense, it was a contrast to my blackness-loving home. My mother immigrated to the United States from Puerto Rico with me in her belly. She was raised in the Ayala Family, well-known as artists who hold up what is black and African in Puerto Rican culture. If there is one thing that characterizes the Ayalas, it's their unmitigated love for black people. Hearing my family talk about black Puerto Rican culture, history, and music with passion and reverence made an impression on me. It was as if no one had ever informed them that black people are generally positioned as low status in many societies.

I observed interactions and devoured books. Once I discovered a great author, I read all of her or his books — Toni Morrison, Alice Walker, Richard Wright, Audre Lorde, Gloria Anzaldua, bell hooks, Foucault, Jane Roberts, Gurumayi, Muktananda, Nityananda, Abhinavagupta, to name a few. I eventually identified a core question that drove me through the next few decades: **What is the relationship between the freedom of social change and the liberation of spiritual traditions?**

In college I studied feminist theory and social-change organization-al models. I knew I wanted to work in social change in a praxis way, working in the field and as a thinker, writer, and strategist. My approach has been to move around within the field to better understand how it functions as a system. I have worked in social service agencies, advocacy organizations, grassroots organizing networks, philanthropic founda-tions, a leadership and management firm, and a strategy center. **I have found that social-change agents use the same power frameworks and tools that the dominant use.**

Currently, my professional life is defined by writing and consulting, mostly strategy and innovation. I specialize in network approaches and elegant design. I have a particular interest in social movements, and recent work includes projects with the national leaders of the Black Lives Matter movement and the national immigrant youth movement network, United We Dream.

My spiritual work has always been a part of me but finds its realization in the practice of Siddha Yoga, a spiritual path arising from the teachings of Kashmir Shaivism, considered the highest iteration of spiritual mys-ticism. Kashmir Shaivism affirms the supreme identity of the individual self, the intrinsic connection with the Divine. It offers a powerful model of consciousness.

Finally, this book was greatly influenced by my daughter, Saphia Suarez. She started acting at the age of four in local children's theater programs. Over the years, I drove Saphia to and from numerous classes, rehearsals, and performances. Once, when she was a teenager and had been at it for over 10 years, I went to see a presentation from an acting workshop at Wheelock Family Theater in Boston titled "Theater of the Absurd." The performance was a piece from *Waiting for Godot*, where the two student actors played out a seemingly banal dominant/subordinate interaction in which the subordinate had to find and utilize the moment where the dynamic could be interrupted and transformed. Excitement rose in me as I watched, instantly realizing this kind of thinking and practice as the missing piece in my book. After the performance, I ran up to the teacher and asked her about status and improvisational theater. She recommended Keith Johnstone, the leading acting teacher for this approach. This launched my personal passion for and study of acting as a liberatory practice. My daughter decided to study acting, and as the writing of this book comes to a conclusion, she begins her studies at Yale University's drama department. As we went through the process of college application and selection last year, she told me, "The way you took acting so seriously shifted the way I approached it. It used to be a passion. Now it's my purpose." But it was she who taught me how to take acting seriously.

·····

The Power Manual brings these many experiences and ideas together and explores major concepts of power, with a focus on the dynamics of domination and liberation. It proposes a new theory of power based on enactment — the bringing of something to life through one's actions. The book weaves together thinking from feminist theory, postmodern theory, sociology, psychoanalysis, neuroendocrinology, business management, developmental psychology, political theory, spiritual mysticism, economics, anthropology, and theater. It looks at key ways that power is deployed and transformed so that one may enact freedom.

Key ideas cut across the many aforementioned genres. For example, the fact that difference is a trigger for power dynamics and also a key way that one unconsciously evaluates environmental data, with a bias toward similarity; the critical role that attention plays and that it is also a resource one's body uses sparingly; that interactions structure social systems and are also sites of resistance; the primacy of the two core emotional states of joy and anxiety; and the constant finding that power skills are learnable.

The book has 24 chapters across four sections — identity, choice, thresholds, and games. The first 12 chapters contain a story, key ideas, and frameworks. The last 12 chapters are power games. Ultimately, the role of identity in power dynamics is that of refusing powerless identities and enacting powerful identities. Choice allows one to move away from dominant power interactions, toward egalitarian interactions, but it requires attention, a limited resource. Thresholds, or points of transition, allow one to understand and master the process of power expansion and perceive the everyday points of choice. Games order and reorder interactions with others and the self, and thus are perfect vehicles for learning power relationships.

This approach shifts the focus of the actor to the self, to one's ability to imagine, and one's discipline of attention and effort in the pursuit of freedom. I write in a stripped down, stylized manner, focusing on the core ideas, that allows the tracking of power frameworks and practices across different genres and fields. I place citations for the key writings that influenced my work in a Notes chapter at the end, and focus on my own thinking in the body. This simplifies the chapters and clarifies my contribution to the ideas I weave together. While the subject of power is a complicated one, my aim is to create a book that is sophisticated in its thinking *and* accessible.

·····

Why do power relations matter in social change, or for any of us who care about living the best life we can live? Because we have to be clear about the type of power we seek. We need power to move through the world and construct a meaningful life, but we must ensure that it is liberatory — allowing us to thrive and create the beauty that can come only from who one is now as this incarnated soul, while also ensuring that we do not perpetuate domination.

I am left balancing two truths — that much interaction is based on dominant ways of thinking *and* we are all, essentially, souls in communion, playing out the drama of life with each other. Can we become more conscious of this interplay and, beginning with our actions, create a better world?

Section One

Power + Identity
Refusing Powerless Identities

Power + Identity Intro
Refusing Powerless Identities

W hat is power? And how does one obtain power, especially if one is defined as powerless by society?

There are three core propositions in chapter 1, Effective Interactions, drawing on the work of Michel Foucault and bell hooks: (1) that there are both supremacist and liberatory ways to act out power, (2) that liberatory power is real power, and (3) that one can access liberatory power by fine-tuning one's consciousness. Power is relational; it plays out in interactions. Structures, rules, and systems are the artifacts of our interactions. Therefore, useful liberation practices focus on effective interactions — in which we seek mutuality and egalitarian interactions and refuse powerless identities.

Chapter 2, Interaction Patterns, highlights the thinking of Audre Lorde, Roland Barthes, and Franz Fanon. Lorde identified difference as the key factor that triggers power dynamics, or unequal interactions. Barthes brilliantly revealed that underneath all the various ways that one can assert dominant power (such as racism, sexism, classism), there are actually seven basic dominant interaction patterns, and they are so much a part of rational thinking that they may at first seem benign. They are tolerance, objectification, assimilation, authority, objectivity, accumulation, and certainty. Luckily, Fanon showed that there are also patterns of resistance — sign reading (the ability to see signs of domination), deconstruction (the ability to understand the relationships between signs of domination and the narratives they create that drive interactions), and reconstruction (the ability to rearrange the signs to tell a new, more mutual story).

Chapter 3, Transmission of Affect, focuses on the work of Theresa Brennan, who was my professor at the New School's Feminist Theory

program. Brennan used research from the field of psychoneuroendocrinology, the study of hormones and their relationship to behavior, to
reveal how our hormones act on each other during interactions. This is
called affect. She hints at the role of affect in uneven power relationships
when she writes about how, in society, women carry the disordered
affects of men, or projected aggressions, which women experience as
unwanted aggression that is carried in the body and manifests as anxiety
or depression. This work being done by women lowers the available
energy for living and creating. The book focuses on what affect is and
how it works, but to me, the most important contribution is the main
point of chapter 3 — whether it is done consciously or unconsciously,
the typical interaction between a dominant and a subordinate is one in
which the dominant offloads anxiety and the subordinate uploads that
anxiety. Finally, Brennan offers that a key way to resist negative affect is
through the classical virtues — courage, prudence, temperance, justice,
hope, faith, and love — which she defines in relationship to affect and as
something that is practiced in interactions.

*By this point, I was starting to see convergence around some key ideas: that
the locus of power, the place where it can be transformed, is interactions;
that the way one relates to difference is something one has to contend with
and explore because fear of difference and curiosity about difference trigger
very different interactions; finally, there's the assurance that this is a lifelong
practice, something at which one can constantly work and improve.*

Chapter 4, The Sources of Power Relations, introduces the reality that
the way we relate to power is developmental and that the foundation
starts in childhood, where we learn through our interactions whether we
can get what we want or not. These early interactions with our care-
takers teach us the standards of value, what is valued in one's society.
We move from one developmental level to a higher one by learning to
increasingly integrate experiences of difference.

*This chapter stumped me for a while because I realized that while libera-
tory power and egalitarian interactions could be held up as ideal, in fact, it*

appeared as if only people at high levels of development could function this way in a relatively consistent manner. This made sense when I thought back to the proposition that one could access liberatory power by fine-tuning one's consciousness, but it also seemed that holding this as a general expectation for human interaction may be a bit unrealistic. Further, there was the realization that freedom is not for the faint of heart. It is something one has to live into moment by moment, more akin to spiritual practice than the power struggles central to social movements, more focused on our internal relationship to power than the external ones, which are reflections.

Finally, chapter 5, Powerless and Powerful Identities, explores the space between Gramsci's hegemony, the idea that the very acceptance of power as dominance renders one powerless, and the philosophy of Supreme Power outlined in the ancient Shiva Sutras. It overlaps dominant power (hegemony) and liberatory power (one's inherent Supreme Power) and reiterates the assurance that power is something that we practice and develop, and is a priori available to us by virtue of being a conscious being.

Effective Interactions
Supremacist Power and Liberatory Power

1

*M*ax was one of the first black students admitted into elite private schools on the east coast of the United States. While his parents sent him to these schools to receive a quality education, to make it through, Max also learned to navigate difficult social dynamics. He recalls that, when he was in eighth grade, there was a white student who was always making fun of him. As one of the few black students, Max had been picked on a lot. "A black kid is someone who is clearly different on the outside," Max said. Eventually, Max decided he wasn't going to give this kid any more attention. This annoyed the kid, who tried different ways to regain the upper hand. He eventually began to be nice to Max, in hopes of getting his attention again, to no avail. Their peers noticed this shift in attention — of power — and the kid lost their esteem. Max was learning how to perceive and shift power dynamics.

We all want power. The power to attract the love we want. The power to create what we want to see in the world. The power to avoid harm. But what is power? And how does one obtain power, especially if one is defined as powerless by society, as black people are?

Power is, first of all, relational. It operates in relationships of inequality where we seek advantage and so is intentional. On the other hand, we are lessened by the inability to assert equality of right and opportunity in an interaction. Power is not about the rule of law, institutions, society, or the state. These are simply the dead forms, or artifacts, that result from past power-laden interactions, or confrontations.

Power is exercised, not acquired. Everyday interactions contain aims and objectives that make the exercise of power visible and understandable.

Power is also never absolute. There is always resistance. Power is a force field of relationships based on inequality.

Oftentimes leaders or social-change activists think that, if they create and implement new structures, they can shift the way people in an organization interact. Focusing instead on creating collective understanding of how people are currently interacting and their desired ways of interacting can lead to exponential and immediate change.

For example, Otto Scharmer and Ursula Versteegen worked with a network of physicians in an area of Frankfurt, Germany, to improve emergency care service. They began by conducting over 100 interviews with both patients and physicians. They then invited the people interviewed to share the results. Almost 100 attended.

The interviews revealed four different levels at which patients and physicians could relate. The first level was *transactional*. The patient comes in with a problem, and the physician fixes it. It is like a machine with a broken part that a mechanic repairs. The second level was *behavioral*. Here the physician tells the patient the behavior that has to change, and the patient tries to change it. In the third, the *assumptive*, the physician helps the patient understand the assumptions that underlie the behavior to be changed, and the patient works to question and change the assumptions. In the fourth, the *identity* level, the physician helps the patient understand how the illness may indicate a need to let go of an old identity and explore a new one.

Meeting participants then broke into small groups and talked about what the levels meant to them. They then identified the level(s) that they were currently functioning within and the one(s) they desired. The final tally revealed that both patients and physicians felt they were functioning at levels one and two, and both wanted to function at three and four. They realized that they wanted the same thing and that the system was them, what they chose to enact. With this new awareness, participants spoke about how this was true in their own work and thought of ways they could behave differently. They began to share ideas and went on to work on many projects together, including an innovative emergency care system.

Useful liberation practices focus on effective interactions — interactions that disrupt dominating behavior (the taking of more than one's share) and generate mutuality (practicing reciprocity in relationships). There are two key points regarding effective interactions: (1) one must constantly **refuse powerless identities** in interactions, and (2) one can **build capacity for effective interactions**. It is in everyday interactions that one either contributes to unequal power dynamics or interrupts them.

To assert one's own power in a way that promotes mutuality, one must know the type of power one seeks. There are two fundamental types of power. One is the ability to dominate, or control, people and things. This power rests on relative rank and the privilege of being at the top. It reflects a supremacist way of thinking — an acceptance of relationships of domination and submission. Supremacist power is a crude form of power, related to scarcity consciousness, or the belief that the world holds limited supplies of the things we want — love, power, recognition. An alternative type of power is liberatory power — the ability to create what we want. It stems from abundance consciousness. Liberatory power requires the transformation of what one currently perceives as a limitation. The distinction between these two types of power is important.

People committed to liberation often focus on the domination aspects of power, on understanding the ways some people are made powerless by others. Though there is much to understand about this type of power and how it works, focusing on it often limits the attention to the ways one *does* assert power — a critical aspect of liberatory power.

Further, one can build one's capacity for liberatory power. It requires a commitment to living mindfully, constantly increasing one's level of awareness, so that when one finds oneself in an interaction that positions one as powerless, one is able to perceive it, keep calm, and assert mutuality. Liberatory power helps one refrain from asserting power over others, or to do so carefully.

The stories one tells oneself and others transmit or transmute power. *Max decided not to give his tormentor any more attention. He revised the story to make him insignificant, and it worked.* The story about what is happening shapes reality, particularly whether one is positioned as powerless or powerful in it. Liberatory power invites one to construct a story about oneself as powerful. It trains us to look for where our power is. Over time, one is able to move through the force field of relationships without taking on the low opinion of others or opining low of others.

Thus, there are four core propositions: (1) power is negotiated in interactions; (2) there are supremacist and liberatory ways to act out power; (3) liberatory power is real power; and (4) one can access liberatory power by fine-tuning one's consciousness and increasing one's access to choice.

Questions for Consideration in Interactions

1. What are the most immediate, the most local, power relationships at work?

2. What narrative(s) make this power relationship possible?

3. How is this power relationship linked to other power relationships to form a strategy for dominance?

4. How was the power relationship modified in the interaction, strengthening some terms and weakening others?

Interaction Patterns
Patterns of Domination and Patterns of Resistance

*A*rtemis is a student of power and liberation. As a young girl growing up in a black neighborhood, she learned at an early age to navigate social dangers. She went on to college, and then to graduate school, deepening her knowledge and experience of power and liberation. As she moved into the social-change field, she realized that the fight for liberation is actually a journey toward enlightenment.*

The concept of difference is central to interactions in relationships of inequality. Humans have used differences to value, divide, and structure society — as with race, gender, class, age, and sexuality. One's relationship to difference impacts one's interactions, either reinforcing these structures of value or interrupting them.

The supremacist approach to power offers two options for dealing with difference: ignore it or view it as cause for separation. A liberatory approach views differences as strengths and entertains interdependence as an option. For the dominant, embracing difference requires one to face one's fear of the subordinate, the other, and allow oneself to be changed, grow, and be redefined by one's encounters. For the subordinate, the change that needs to occur in the space between difference and interdependence is a move away from dominant, or supremacist, ways of thinking. These are narratives that position one as powerless.

For Artemis, it turned out that the field of social change was a perfect arena for the study of power and liberation. One way she saw the fear of difference show up in even this work was in the demand for shared analysis and strategies for social change. Rather than the civic engagement and policy practitioners being happy for and working with the civil disobedience

15

activist, they critiqued them and dismissed them as people who did not yet know how things really worked.

Once, Artemis was in Worcester, a town an hour away from Boston, her hometown, working on the electoral campaign of a white man running for state representative. It was a comfortable fall day, and she was told by the leaders at the campaign office that she had an easy district to canvass, a progressive neighborhood overwhelmingly in support of her candidate. As the day was coming to an uneventful end, Artemis, on the last block on her list, the clipboard in her hand, saw a young white family get out of a pickup truck that had just pulled into a driveway up ahead. She looked, hesitant to walk over and talk to them, but the woman waved Artemis over to ask about her candidate. It turned out that she was working on the opponent's team and was curious about the messages her candidate was putting out on Artemis's candidate. As Artemis listened to the issues that she cared about framed so negatively, she thought about how to engage this woman, who was spitting with conviction as she talked, ready to defend her beliefs. The woman went on to say that she and her husband, to whom she gestured, had worked hard to buy their house and raise a child, who toddled nearby, in contrast to a friend she had who cheated the system. This friend didn't work and "figured out" ways to get subsidized housing and food. The woman said she could imagine that there were more people like her friend, riding on the backs of hard-working people like herself and her husband. Artemis noted the tension rising in her body and realized she was anxious. She was not used to talking to someone with this perspective. Though a woman of color, she lived in a bubble of college-educated, racially diverse, social-change practitioners and activists. Clearly, Artemis and this woman both wanted the same things — safety, adequate resources, and the ability to pursue personal happiness.

Finally, the words came: "I am glad that the system worked for you and your family, but it didn't work for me. My husband happened to be Arab, and though he went to college, had a good job, and worked hard, after September 11 he had to leave the country, and now my daughter, who is about the same age as your son," she said, pointing to the little guy beside her, "doesn't see her father much because he is exiled in Canada." The woman's eyes widened, clearly taking in new information. "So my candidate is lying to me?" she asked, considering the implications of this new understanding. "These are people just like me, trying to make it work?" "Yes," said Artemis. The woman thanked Artemis, looking troubled, and promised to look further into it. As Artemis walked away, noticing the thumping of her heart, she realized that that had been the most exhilarating moment of the day. She had walked to the periphery of her world and managed to make contact on the other side. She felt expanded, bigger, lighter. She walked down the street, turned, and climbed the stairs of her candidate's campaign office. As she walked in and excitedly shared her experience with some of the other campaigners returning from their two-hour shifts, she quickly noticed their looks and felt herself retreat into herself as one of them, a young white man, said, "You did it all wrong! You're not supposed to talk to the enemy!"

Effective interactors know how to cross thresholds of difference. One can deepen the practice of effective interactions by understanding and identifying key interaction patterns of domination and liberation. A pattern is a combination of qualities, acts, and tendencies that form a consistent or characteristic arrangement. Anyone can use patterns of domination, regardless of race, class, gender, or other difference. These are like masks one is invited to wear, innocent-seeming ways of thinking that support relationships of domination. What triggers them is an encounter with difference. They reflect an inability to make room for the other. They are used not only by the obedient citizen but also the rebellious social-change agent. There are seven interaction patterns of domination.

The first, and fundamental, pattern is *tolerance*. In this interaction, one allows small doses of difference — enough to stimulate but not enough to require change. Tolerance demands moderation. This shows up in organizations that strive for diversity instead of equity. The concept of diversity flows from a supremacist perspective. It is framed as a value to the dominant. It adds nuance to a situation, but it does not change the relationships of power.

The second pattern is *objectification*. Here one removes history from the interaction so as to avoid responsibility for what happened and will happen. Imagine one is a first-world citizen vacationing in third-world country, simply appreciating the beauty of the place and friendly locals. One basks in the privilege that allows one to consume in this way and suffers no recognition of the cost the locals have paid and are paying. One feels no personal responsibility for the past and does not see how one contributes to the condition in the present.

The third domination pattern is *assimilation* — one is incapable of seeing difference. The other is a version of oneself gone astray. This allows one to ignore difference by reducing it to sameness. If one cannot completely ignore the difference, one deems it exotic. While this may seem like a compliment, it defines the other as foreign and unknowable. This occurs when one is not able to be curious when faced with a different interpretation of reality. Instead of seeking to understand how or why this reality makes sense to the other, one seeks to make the other see the "truth" and correct behavior.

In the fourth pattern, *authority*, rationality is hidden. Something is because one says it is so. One does not have to justify it or provide explanations. The simplest example is the parent who responds to a child's "Why?" with "Because I said so!"

Objectivity is the fifth. Here one ignores power-laden realities, believing one is taking the higher ground. This is reflected in the much-valued claim of neutrality that characterizes the dominant psyche. It is noncommitted, detached, and moderate, as when one says, "I will not hire someone based on the color of their skin. I will hire the best." It is this very levelheadedness that creates the inflexibility that supports the dominant order. One does not take into account the reality that racial histories have underdeveloped whole groups of people and given other groups unearned advantages.

The sixth pattern, *accumulation*, refers to the collecting of experiences and things. Quantity is made to stand in for quality. More is better, and he who has the most wins. An example is deferential treatment for the wealthy simply because they are wealthy and regardless of the quality of being. Or, conversely, dismissive treatment of a subordinate, regardless of the quality of being, simply because of lower status.

Finally, there is *certainty* — when one asserts one's reality as if there is no other. One knows for sure and speaks in declarative sentences. One sets the frame for the interaction, expecting the other to slide into one's narrative. It is devised to make one's reality the operative one. One must unlearn this fetish of assertion. Refraining from assertiveness is the discipline to make space for looking into another person's life and for the other to look equally into one's life.

Learning to live with people who differ is one of the most urgent challenges facing societies today. These seven domination patterns — tolerance, objectification, assimilation, authority, objectivity, accumulation, and certainty — are considered acceptable and encouraged in postmodern Western societies, but they do not help us live well together. Patterns of domination make one rigid and keep one from fuller forms of existence. In order to wear these masks, one must disconnect from authentic experiences, which are mutual.

Patterns of Domination

1.	Tolerance	Small doses of difference are allowed
2.	Objectification	Removes history from the interaction
3.	Assimilation	Incapable of seeing difference
4.	Authority	Rationality is hidden
5.	Objectivity	Ignores power-laden realities
6.	Accumulation	Quantity stands in for quality
7.	Certainty	Asserting one's reality as if there is no other

As there are patterns of domination, there are also patterns of resistance. These are ways of being that disrupt relationships of power by making space for the other. They require a freedom from archetypes and the capacity to try on new ways of thinking. Just as one has the choice to rigidify, one also has the choice to endlessly recreate oneself.

We develop in relationship. This is a cross-racial, cross-class, cross-nation existence. It is interstitial being, a reconnecting across boundaries, in two senses. One, it is living between one's reality and another's. Two, it is living between one's present self and one's future self. Disrupting relationships of power requires one to redirect one's life energy away from patterns of domination and toward cocreating new, mutual realities.

Learning to live between worldviews allows one to disrupt the dominant realities of monocultures and see the narratives to which one has become acculturated. There are three interaction patterns of resistance. They are three types of powers that together help one make space for new realities.

Sign reading is the power to see and feel the often-invisible signs of patterns of domination, such as the ones outlined above. It is the ability to understand the ways one structures meaning in a way that carries power. The dominance approach is related to the rule of men and the overvaluation of masculine characteristics. It is in relationship with accumulation. It relies on individuality, or the lack of relationship to others, the past, and the future. It uses aggression to address conflict. Understanding the symbols of dominant power narratives is the power of sign reading.

Deconstruction is the power to understand how the signs of power come together to construct narratives that support particular power arrangements. For example, it is being able to understand how the signs outlined above — dominance, overvalued masculinity, accumulation, individuality, aggression — together create and sustain patriarchal societies. Patriarchal societies are imbalanced societies. They subordinate the feminine powers of creation, care, and relationship, which build society and culture. Ancient symbols like the yin/yang remind us of the ancient wisdom of the balance of destruction and creation.

Reconstruction is the power to rearrange the signs to tell a different story, to create new realities from the elements of the current one. One looks for overlooked or suppressed ways of thinking that are significant in the situation. Since power is never absolute, there are always submerged narratives ready to emerge. In patriarchal societies, invoking the feminine contributes to balance and mutuality.

Patterns of resistance require a commitment to egalitarianism, the belief in the equality of all people. It maintains that all individuals are equal in fundamental worth. It predisposes one toward mutuality in interactions, the give and take of ideas and feelings such that all are altered by the interaction.

A commitment to egalitarianism results in the acceptance of living in a state of constant expansion. One doesn't take on the low opinion of others and strives to think well of others. One becomes more multifaceted with every interaction. It enables a different sense of control.

Patterns of Resistance

Sign Reading	The power to see signs of patterns of domination
Deconstruction	The power to understand the relationships between the signs of patterns of domination
Reconstruction	The power to use signs to tell a different, more mutual, story

We live and experience power in relationships, within interactions. Understanding patterns of domination helps one cut through the details and identify the core interaction patterns that prevent mutuality. One's main task is to disrupt these patterns of domination in one's interactions, whether they arise from the other or oneself.

Transmission of Affect
Life-affirming and Life-draining Affects

At the end of the film *The Taking of Power by Louis XIV*, the young king says,

> There is a loftiness that does not come from fortune. It's a certain air of superiority which seems to destine us for greatness. It's a prize that we give to ourselves imperceptibly. It's by virtue of this quality that we usurp the deference of other men, and it is this which places us above them more than birth, dignity, or even merit.

Recent research in the field of psychoneuroendocrinology, the study of hormones and their relationship to behavior, revealed that our hormones act on each other during interactions. What one feels about another is transmitted in one's interaction and affects the other's biological body. Like genes, memes are units of influencing information. While genes are currently understood as contained, traveling only down the biological line, memes are not contained. These units of meaning travel sideways, transmitted through interactions, challenging the Darwinian assumption of self-containment. This phenomenon is called affect: the act of producing an effect or change in another, in body, feelings, or mind.

Affect is perceived passively as a bodily emotion caused by another or the environment, in that the environment holds the signals we send each other. Some of this is not new. The concept of entrainment, the tendency of people to fall into synchronicity with each other, has been around for some time. Affect narrows the window down to microinteractions. The small day-to-day interactions with others that shape us.

In understanding affect, the heart is key. Pheromones are olfactory molecules that carry one's intentions and act as direction givers. They travel between people through space. What one feels in one's heart is communicated to another via the sense of smell. The other picks up this information, mostly unconsciously. In turn, the hormonal intentions of others can enter one's body and influence, leading one to accept another's intention as one's own, again, often unaware. This challenges the assumption that intentionality has to be conscious.

Affect has two main states that are reflected in the body: anxiety and joy. Anxiety becomes stress and illness, and joy becomes well-being and health. Thus, anxiety diminishes one's life power, and joy enhances it. People toggle back and forth between anxiety and joy, seeking to minimize anxiety and maximize joy.

An interaction that triggers anxiety, a threat response, is emotionally overwhelming and mentally taxing. It lowers one's personal productivity because it diverts and uses up oxygen and glucose, which would otherwise go toward other, more creative, uses. However, research in this field has also observed the plasticity of the brain, its capacity to remold, to recreate itself. This means that with attention and intention one can learn to respond to threats with something other than anxiety.

The human brain is social. One is constantly assessing how interactions either enhance or diminish one's status because, in the dominant, or supremacist, worldview, status is associated with the ability to get the things one needs: love, power, and recognition. Low status is associated with exclusion. When one feels excluded, one's body exhibits the same neurological activity exhibited during physical pain. There is heightened activity in the part of the brain that signals suffering. The more one feels excluded, the higher the level of brain activity. Realizing that one might compare unfavorably to someone else causes anxiety to kick in, releasing cortisol and other stress-related hormones. Feelings of low status induce cortisol levels similar to chronic anxiety. To be low status is to live in a state of chronic anxiety. Conversely, high status correlates with health. Affects, thus, have a regulatory function, helping biological organisms move away from death and toward optimal living.

One maintains one's sense of self by projecting onto others the affects that interfere with one's sense of ability to act, such as any sense of inferiority and the anxiety it invokes. Offloading anxiety increases the likelihood of joy for the offloader. These affective judgments are, in turn, usually uploaded by the other. **Whether it is done consciously or unconsciously, the typical interaction between a dominant and a subordinate is one where the dominant offloads anxiety and the subordinate uploads that anxiety.** Therefore, one's status in society overdetermines how much anxiety one is likely to upload.

When uploading anxiety, one is driven by an intention that is not one's own. The state of being subordinate is one in which one is more likely to show stress symptoms than others and less likely to have the opportunity to offload. Further, affects have a cumulative effect. The fewer the negative aspects around one, the easier it is to resist them. The more there are, the harder it is.

Affect is a major site of struggle. Resistance is always a choice. Resistance begins with the ability to recognize, engage, and redirect affect. This ability is a core source of power. It is an ability that can be learned.

First, one must learn to note the arrival of an affect in order to understand its pathway. One does this through identifying and exploring impulses. Affect begins with an impulse. An impulse is both a sudden urge that prompts an unpremeditated act and (over time) an inclination. If one follows one's impulses without reflection, one will not be able to notice, much less change, the direction of the pathway. One can learn to have choice — to engage the impulse or to let it take one for a ride. There is a choice to be made between being active and passive, between choosing one's behavior and unconsciously engaging in dominant/subordinate power interactions. It is worth noting that one may also consciously choose to engage in dominant/subordinate interactions for exploration, balance, and pleasure, as with those who practice bondage, domination, sadism, and masochism (BDSM).

The ability to resist affect also requires discernment, the ability to distinguish between one's own feelings and another's affect. Feelings are sensory states produced by thoughts and articulated in words. Awareness of sensory sensation and the ability to put those sensations into words are necessary for feelings. One's feelings have a logic that one can discern. Affects, on the other hand, are interrupting thoughts — thoughts that come from one's environment, as opposed to emanating from within, as feelings do. Discernment also helps one distinguish between the pleasurable and the painful, which helps one understand the difference between life-affirming and life-draining affects.

Finally, an affect can be overcome by a contrary, stronger affect. Overcoming another's affect depends on one's ability to focus one's attention. One's attention is the currency with which one purchases the life one wants. The practice of intentionally directing one's affect is supported by the seven classical virtues, which are a spiritual form of liberatory social codes.

The Classical Virtues

Courage	The strength to resist affect
Prudence	The conservation of energy
Temperance	The strength to resist directing negative affect
Justice	Taking and giving what is appropriate
Hope	The belief that the future can be better
Faith	The assumption that one is the focus of a divine, loving intelligence
Love	A unifying energy

Love reorders aggression. Therefore, negative affects can be deconstructed and reconstructed with love. To love, to resist domination, is to remove oneself from negative affect loops. There is no clearer path to freedom.

Freedom is the ability to be free of negative affects, one's own and those of another. Living freely is refusing to take on another's negative affect. Living responsibly is refusing to project negative affect onto others. Justice is taking no more affect than is appropriate for one's actions and giving the affect that is appropriate for what one receives from another.

Finally, while social codes provide direction, the practices of discernment are comparison, recollection and memory, and detachment. At first one may redirect affect in retrospect, as one reflects over interactions, discerns what one brought to it and what the other did, and thinks about how one might interact differently in the future. Over time, one recognizes affect as it unfolds, which increases one's chances of redirecting it. One learns to have choice in interactions.

Questions for Consideration in Responding with Feelings

1. What am I feeling?
2. Where did this feeling come from?
3. When did it start?
4. What was happening at the time?
5. How is it connected to past events?
6. What are my choices now?

The Sources of Power Relations

Developmental Stages and Mind Forms

A s a little girl, Ava lived in a brownstone apartment across from the Boston Ballet in Boston's South End. Back then that area was home to many working-class families. At school, one of the few white students, Heather, a skinny, blond, wavy-haired girl, talked about her dance classes. After school, Ava could see the practicing Boston Ballet dancers through her window. She thought she would like to try dance and asked her mom if she could take dance classes across the street. Her mom said, "Sure honey. If you can figure out how to get in, I'll take you." Ava remembers this response because it surprised her at the time. She thought her mother would figure things out. What her mother said, though, told her something about how her mother saw her — as someone who could figure this out and, by extension, could make her way through the world. She never did take those dance classes, but she has carried this message of competence with her through life.

One learns about power as a child, through one's interactions with other people. As a child, there were two things one sought in one's interactions with others: control over one's reality and affectionate connection. For example, if one's mother beamed at one, helped one, encouraged one to explore the world, and provided safety and love, then one may feel that the world is a relatively safe place where one can expect to make connection, get one's needs met, and be loved. If, however, one's mother barely gave one attention, except to reprimand, or worse, if she publicly humiliated one, one may feel the world is not a very safe place and that one should be careful and not expect others to be kind.

Interactions also teach standards of value. Since age is one of the many ways that status is assigned in society — along with sex, race, class, and ability — as a child, one became aware of valuations of difference. As one grew, one also learned the corresponding expected ways of acting, or the range within which one could act.

One goes through stages of development. **In each stage, one learns how to interact with and integrate experiences, or not.** Each developmental stage is accompanied by a crisis to be overcome. However, successful completion of each stage is not guaranteed. Unresolved crises bind psychic energy to the past. The child whose parents did not give her what she asked for may be used to not having her needs met. Her behaviors as an adult may then be suited to that condition. Following are the early development stages, where one first learns about power and creates one's power story — the sense of oneself as powerful or powerless.

In the first stage, between birth and 18 months, the crisis was *trust versus mistrust*. One learned that one was distinct from the external environment. One had to figure out whether other people would hear and respond adequately to one's needs. One's ability to have one's needs met in relationships fostered trust in the external world; and one's inability, mistrust.

The second stage, between two to three years of age, was characterized by the crisis of *autonomy versus shame*. One developed a sense of what one wanted and whether one could get it. One learned about the setting of boundaries. This is what the two-year-old's "no" is about. The power to refuse includes the power to limit one's own desires in response to another's "no." If one was encouraged to assert one's will, one learned to negotiate one's boundaries. If one was discouraged, one may have learned to choose between denying one's feelings and denying external realities. The development of language, which happened in relationship, impacted one's ability to engage with one's environment in a manner that helped one get what one wanted, or not. Language, then, is a tool of power.

Between three to five years of age, *initiative versus guilt*, one attempted to link one's will to a goal. One's ability to imagine a desired future and then attain it reinforced one's developing identity as powerful. If one experienced the ability to initiate activity, one learned that one could make decisions and engage others — that one could sometimes be a leader. If one was not able to engage others in one's initiatives, one may have felt embarrassed, guilty of being only a follower.

In summary, if as a child one's development was nurtured and supported, by the age of five, one learned that one could have one's needs heard and answered, that one had a will and could assert it, and that one could create one's future and thus oneself. One learned a healthy sense of power. If not, one learned that one cannot count on getting one's needs met through relationships with others, that one cannot assert one's will easily, and that it is not easy to imagine a desired future, or goal, and attain it.

EARLY DEVELOPMENTAL STAGES			
Stage	Age	Crisis	Experience
First	Birth to 18 Months	Trust vs Mistrust	Does the external world respond to one's needs?
Second	2 to 3 Years	Autonomy vs Shame	Is one able to assert one's will?
Third	3 to 5 Years	Initiative vs Guilt	Is one able to imagine a desired future and attain it?

Between the age of five and transition to young adulthood, around 18, one solidified one's ability to attain one's goals and identity, particularly in terms of relationships to others and life purpose, or work. If this development was successful, one developed a healthy ego identity, a strong sense of self. One learned to experience oneself as competent and worthy of attention, and even love.

As an adult, there are other identities beyond ego identity. Moving through them requires the ability to integrate increasing complexity, or difference. The identities are referred to as mind forms, or forms of mind, ways of making sense of the world. As with the developmental stages, one will not automatically move through the four mind forms. At each form, one has the choice to stay or do the work of leaping to the next, bigger form.

To understand mind forms, it helps to differentiate between informational learning, or learning within your current mind form, and transformational learning, learning beyond one's current mind form. Informational learning is learning that helps one learn new data. It is about increasing the content one has. Transformational learning is learning that changes how one thinks about the content one already has. Moving through life forms requires transformational learning.

With the *self-sovereign mind form*, one's beliefs and feelings remain constant over time. One understands that others have their own preferences and perspectives, but one cannot make sense of them. One has not yet learned to make sense of one's own. One manages complexity with black-and-white decisions and cannot see shades of gray. One is motivated by self-interest. One follows rules to avoid punishment. When rules do not serve one's interests, one will break them, if possible. One does not think about one's inner workings and, when angry or afraid, is likely to locate the cause externally and lash out at another. The learning edge, or learning beyond comfort zone, is integrating with society.

As one begins to increase awareness of others' perspectives, one begins to transition into the *socialized mind form*. With this form, one begins to subordinate one's perspective, or will, to that of the group, as one begins to move toward affiliation and expertise. One can get enough distance from the self to see a bigger picture that includes others. This introduces gray into the previous black-and-white decision-making frame. While this can be exciting, it can also be overwhelming. One finds guidance in external theories and internalizes those one trusts. They are a buffer against the temporary anxiety caused by the uncertainty that accompanies a wider frame. One follows the rules not to avoid consequences, but because one believes in them and wants to belong. When one is angry or afraid, one can name the emotion and see it as the cause for any lashing out. One does not feel control over the emotion and feels subject to the other, whom one believes caused the emotion. The learning edge is moving from external theories to a more personal set of beliefs.

When one begins to question the ideas one had previously assumed, one begins the path toward the *self-authored mind form*. This is the most common mind form, found in older adolescents and the majority of adults. With it one can hold many different perspectives and make informed decisions driven by one's own values. One does not need other people to help make sense of the world. One has crafted a personal philosophy. One knows what one values and relies on an internal judgment system. One believes that if one works hard enough, one can create a system big enough to hold all of the complexity one experiences. When angry or afraid, one notices the self's role in creating this response, is able to not get caught up in the emotion, and can instead reflect on one's reaction. The learning edge is extreme complexity, such as cross-cultural or cross-functional situations — situations that require one to examine one's value system.

Many adults do not live their way into the self-authored mind, and far fewer make it to the *self-transforming mind form*. With it, one has learned the limits of the self-authored mind. One understands that the previous mind forms reflect the development of an inner system with a focus on difference, and that this itself is the problem, and begins to move beyond difference. Now one sees the similarities that are hidden inside differences. Instead of focusing on difference, one sees connections everywhere.

There is always more reality than that which one allows. One decides the boundaries of one's life. This is where freedom comes in. Power is learned, and, thus, can always be modified.

MIND FORMS			
Type	Self	Other	Development
Self-sovereign	Constant beliefs and feelings	Cannot make sense of other perspectives	Increasing awareness of others' perspectives
Socialized	Can take distance from constant self	Can take on the perspectives of others	Beginning to question assumptions
Self-authored	Has many perspectives	Cannot hold the competing values of others	Seeing limits of self-authoring
Self-transforming	Sees inner system based on difference as the problem	Sees connections everywhere	Unknown

Powerless and Powerful Identities
Hegemony and Supreme Power

5

C leo had a black male colleague named Vincent who was a vice president at the firm. Vincent had a small team made up of black and
*Latinx staff. He was highly paid, reported directly to the CEO, and talked
a lot about being powerless as a black man. From where Cleo, also black,
stood, as a director a level below him, Vincent had a lot of power. She found
that by proposing direction and solutions to the challenges the new firm
faced, she could significantly influence it. One day, at a tense meeting, as
the firm considered significant downscaling, Vincent spoke to a small team
of people of color about what was happening and how they could protect
themselves. The room was tense, as staff worried about losing their jobs.
Cleo suggested that they instead focus on the power they did have, which
was significant. After all, the firm was more than 50 percent people of color,
and they had a lot of ideas about what it could be doing. She felt Vincent's
leadership was an obstacle and contributed to the firm's ultimate closure.
She understood that, though Vincent had role power, he did not have a
powerful identity. Conversely, while she did not always have significant role
power, she found ways to be powerful no matter what the circumstances.*

In the postmodern age in which we live, we hear that power relations
have evolved from domination into hegemony — the social, cultural,
ideological, or economic influence exerted by a dominant group, to
which one may or may not belong. The core idea is that that which
is to be challenged or resisted already lives within. One is, in a sense,
rendered powerless to resist a priori. Hegemony offers a powerless
identity.

Italian Marxist Antonio Gramsci is credited with popularizing the term
hegemony. He came to the word in his effort to revise socialist ideology

in the wake of unexpected losses. It was 1926, and he concluded that socialism had been defeated. The extant Marxist theory of change was that economic crisis would lead to political reform — but this had not occurred. Gramsci noted that the system was somehow able to absorb the conflict, and he sought to understand how this worked.

Gramsci's new philosophy was that change was produced not so much by changing socioeconomic circumstances, or what he called structures, but by relations of force at the political and ideological level, or superstructures, which he equated with hegemony. For example, while employers and those who work for them constantly seek ways to make employees work more for less, since wages are generally seen as a negotiation site for increasing profit, employees are faced with the weakening of unions, the disappearance of jobs to other countries where wages are lower, and the persistent idea that the key to success is hard work and a college degree. Superstructures are the institutions and culture that support a society's economic system. They enable widespread control.

Gramsci sought to understand relationships of domination at the social level. Marxist thought had, until then, focused on economic power, with the assumption that it would impact political and ideological power. Gramsci proposed that perhaps power flowed in the opposite direction, from ideological and political power to economic power. What is accepted as true and knowable is shaped by those who have the power to make their interpretation of reality hold — the domination pattern of certainty described in chapter 2, Interaction Patterns — that in turn affects how resources are distributed in society.

Gramsci's new philosophy started with the assertion that superstructures are an objective and operative reality and, as such, are knowable. One can access them by becoming conscious of one's way of being in society and overall process of becoming. In other words, through discernment — or comparison, recollection, memory, and detachment — that supports active choice.

For Gramsci, social groups that are one hundred percent homogeneous offer the best possibility for revolution. In fact, Gramsci measured the strength of a group's political organization by its degree of homogeneity. Thus, he identified difference as the key problem in the development of political and ideological power.

Though Gramsci views difference as a disadvantage for those seeking political and ideological power, he proclaims the big difference between his philosophy and others' to be that his does not seek to reconcile differences. Instead, he suggests that we learn to live with, or around, difference. Gramsci notes that his is not a philosophy that can be used as a governing tool, which seeks to manage or hide contradictions, but is itself a theory of contradictions, a theory of the governed, in an ongoing journey to self-governance. For him, the key area of analysis is the relationship between structure and superstructure, or between economic systems and the political and ideological systems that enable them.

For Gramsci, hegemony is the ultimate stage of domination, beyond the duality of dominant/subordinate relations. **In hegemony**, one has internalized the dominant ideology. **One is powerless because one has internalized the idea of power as dominance.** He defines hegemony as interlocking systems of power that coopt everything to create an integral reality in which there is consensus, whether voluntary or involuntary. Hegemony insists on universality, by which it means Western culture but only the privileged minority, the modern intelligentsia, who sees itself as edifying humanity.

Hegemony constructs a virtual reality apart from the real conditions of power. It activates authority, one of the patterns of domination described in chapter 2, Interaction Patterns. Reality is what those who have captured authority say it is, because it works for them. Such as when Israelis insist that they are the victims of Palestinian "terrorists," while it is they who occupy Palestinian territory by claiming that the land is theirs because they lived there years ago. Further, the United States supports Israel, even though a similar argument by Native Americans would be perceived as laughable because they do not have the ability to enforce it. Hegemony results in growing discrimination, the creation of two different worlds. The hyperreal world of the privileged is beyond reality, while the infrareal world of the dominated is below reality.

The strategies for resisting hegemony are different from those for resisting domination. While domination could be overthrown from outside, hegemony can be only inverted from the inside. A practice of freedom includes both the refusal to be dominated and the refusal to dominate.

One way out of the contradictions (such as the one Gramsci walks around, difference) at one level of reality is to move to a higher, or deeper, level of reality. To better understand how power works at this higher or deeper level, we turn to the philosophy of **Supreme Power** outlined in the Shiva Sutras of ancient India. It **is a philosophy of complete powerfulness, a practice of supreme identity.**

The Shiva Sutras, the philosophy of ancient India, laid out not just **a framework for understanding reality** but also **rules of conduct.** The Shaiva philosophy of Kashmir, considered by many to be the most advanced and integrative version of Supreme Power, is referred to as the philosophy of the triad, referring to

1. Shiva   Identity beyond difference — the highest
2. Shakti   Identity among difference
3. Nara   Soul bound by difference

The Shiva Sutra is considered to be the most important agama, or doctrine, of Shaiva philosophy because it is seen to counter the effects of dualism, or difference, identified as the core limiting condition of the human subject. Its origin is debated, but it is generally accepted that it did not have a human author and instead was revealed to Vasugupta — a Siddha, or "perfected semi divine being" — by Shiva in the late 8th or early 9th century AD. Its purpose is to awaken the mind to pure thoughts about the self. The Shiva Sutra spans four topics.

Ultimate Reality	Nonrelational, beyond form
Manifestation	36 levels of reality
Bondage	The limitation of will, knowledge, and action
Liberation	Recognition of true, Shiva, nature

According to the Shiva Sutras, Ultimate Reality is nonrelational, imme-diate consciousness, with no distinction of subject and object, of self and other. It is the divine energy that creates form. Manifestation, or the world process, the journey from consciousness to materiality, outlines 36 levels of reality. The very nature of Ultimate Reality is to manifest, to create material reality. The first five levels are collectively referred to as the level of *universal experience*. It is the divine unveiled. They are

1. Shiva   Initial, creative movement
2. Shakti   Creates subject and object
3. Will   Consciousness of both subject and object
4. I Am This   Beginning of distinct experience
5. I and This   Distinct self experienced as part of the whole

The second level is referred to as *limited individual experience*. This is where the divine becomes veiled. It is also considered the impure order of illusion. It begins with

6. Maya   Creates particular experience, or difference, by severing the self from the whole

Maya creates the five *Kancukas*, or coverings:

7. Limitation of Efficacy   Moving away from universal authorship
8. Limitation of Knowledge   Moving away from omniscience
9. Limitation of Satisfaction   Moving toward the desire for particular things
10. Limitation of Time   Division of past, present, future

11. Limitation of Cause	Reduction of freedom and Universal Consciousness Space, Form

Then come the levels of reality of the *limited individual*:

12. Individual Subject	Subjective experience of Shiva
13. Matrix of Objectivity	Objective experience of Shiva

The *matrix of objectivity*, in turn, is made up of three genetic constituents, called the three gunas.

Matrix of Objectivity			
Guna	Being	Psychological	Ethical
Sattva	Lightness	Joy	Goodness
Rajas	Activity	Passion	Ambition
Tamas	Inertia	Dullness	Degradation

In unmanifested state, the three gunas, or qualities of nature, sattva, rajas, and tamas — lightness, activity, and inertia — are held in perfect equipoise. In lived experience, or manifestation, however, one or two often predominate.

The levels of *mental operation* are

14. Buddhi	The ability to ascertain, to create an internal mental image that reflects the external object
15. Ahamkara	The I making principle and the power of self appropriation
16. Manas	Sense perception

The five powers of sense perception, the level of *sensible experience*, are

17. Smelling

18. Tasting

19. Seeing
20. Feeling by Touch
21. Hearing

The five powers of action are

22. Speaking
23. Handling
24. Locomotion
25. Excreting
26. Sexual Action and Restfulness

The five *primary elements of perception* are

27. Sound
28. Touch
29. Color
30. Flavor
31. Odor

At the level of *materiality*, we have

32. Space
33. Air
34. Fire
35. Water
36. Earth

These stages of manifestation range from the higher to the subtle to gross materiality. Each tattva is more refined in nature than the next, lower tattva, which is more polluted and extrinsic. Just as one travels down the levels to form and experience embodied reality, one can, and eventually must, travel back up to the state of Shiva, or Unimpeded Sovereignty.

Einstein once said that one cannot solve problems at the level at which they were created. That is, one cannot use the same thinking to solve the problem as was used to create the problem. These stages of manifestation give us a sense of the ancient truth inherent in this insight. If difference is the factor that triggers domination, then rising above difference to identify the similarities beyond it is a path beyond domination.

Further, the Shiva Sutras identify bondage — the limitation of will, knowledge, and action — as a key feature of human experience.

The Aspects of Bondage

Primary Limiting Condition	Contraction from universal consciousness to limited creature
Maya	The illusion of difference
Karma	The residual traces of past desire influenced actions

Liberation is the purpose of existence. Liberation is the recognition of one's true nature, which is Shiva Consciousness. It requires one to replace the false ego experience with the experience of the real Self, to move from relational consciousness to nonrelational consciousness. There are three levels of liberation that one must move up through until one reaches the highest state.

The Levels of Liberation

Shiva Consciousness	Being at one with the Universe, choiceless awareness
Shakti Consciousness	The mind has internalized the sacred
Limited Consciousness	The mind is fixed on an external sacred object considered different from the self

One moves up — from Limited Consciousness based on difference to Shiva Consciousness focused on oneness — through self-effort and Divine grace. For those who believe in divinity, it can be said that self-effort begets Divine grace, the gift of oneness from the Shiva

Consciousness level that must be earned. For those at a more material-
istic level, self-effort makes possible a falling away of the limited self that
allows one's virtuous nature to shine through.

Chapter 3, Transmission of Affect, details how one toggles between
the two core states of anxiety and joy. Here the understanding of that
dichotomy is deepened with the realization that one's natural state is
one of divinity, of Supreme joy, and anxiety is an ontological condition
resulting from contraction, the descent into material reality. All mun-
dane anxiety rests on this core feeling of separation from the divine. At
the same time, Supreme joy is always there, pulling at one with a mag-
netic force.

One experiences only the amount of Divine grace that one is capable
of receiving. Each level of liberation suggests a means of approach for
earning grace. At the level of Limited Consciousness, one externalizes
the sacred and then worships it. As one enters Shakti Consciousness,
one internalizes the sacred. Here one sees that one is the source of
one's own reality, and begins a process of self-inquiry. The focus is on
refining the mind. The highest level of liberation one can achieve is
Shiva Consciousness, in which one is at one with the entire universe
and choice is unnecessary, as there is no difference and no outside. One
accepts what is and sees the power of creation and divinity in it.

However, it is difficult to grasp a higher consciousness from a lower one.
One practice on the path of liberation is meditation on unity consciousness, where there is no difference between the knower, knowledge, and
the known. This is helped by the concept *neti neti* — not this, not this —
where one gets to one's true source by identifying what it is not. It is
a process of removing barriers. When one moves beyond duality to
choiceless awareness, one no longer accepts or rejects but instead lives
in a state of alert passivity. One moves beyond the experience of difference to the experience of seeing the Divine in everyone and everything.
Alert passivity means being on the lookout for the Divine in each other
and responding passively to the triggers of difference. Supreme Identity

is understanding everything, including the self, as divine. One achieves Supreme Identity by purifying one's consciousness, by moving beyond the illusion of difference.

Key Liberation Practices

1.	Meditation on Unity Consciousness	No difference between the knower, knowledge, and the known
2.	Neti Neti	Not this, not this — identifying what is not the true source
3.	Alert Passivity	Being alert to the Divine in the other and passive to difference

Power + Choice

Triggering Choice

Power + Choice Intro
Triggering Choice

H ow does the development of liberatory power through the fine-tuning of one's consciousness, particularly in interactions, work?

Chapter 6, Decision and Choice, introduces the idea that the key lever in interactions is choice, the power to choose for oneself and, very carefully, others — more broadly, the ability to make decisions that are for the good of all. It then describes just how difficult this can be and differentiates between decision making and choice by highlighting the recent research in decision making, the work of Amos Tversky and Daniel Kahneman, which won the Nobel Prize in Economics and replaced the rational agent model. Their main finding was that humans do not make most decisions rationally. Instead decision making is divided across two systems. System 1 is a hidden, unconscious process characterized by intuition and impulses. Decisions are made through trial and error. System 1 seeks to preserve energy and uses shortcuts based on prior experiences, often substituting a difficult question for an easier one to which it already has the answer. Most decisions are made this way, and it works most of the time. When a problem cannot be resolved in System 1, it breaks through to System 2, which is characterized by self-control and the ability to compare among alternatives and choose. This is the space of conflict resolution and conscious processing of difference. However, self-control requires a lot of energy, essentially glucose, and is used sparingly. Building on Tversky and Kahneman's thinking, I conclude that decision making is unconscious and choice is conscious. While they use the terms interchangeably and the field they are in is called decision making, not choice, to me there is a difference.

This was an interesting discovery for me, the fact that the energy we use is essentially glucose, which we have to work hard on a daily basis to produce.

It made me realize just how precious our energy is and how attention to something is use of this energy, so we must be prudent about that to which we give our attention. It is our currency in the world, particularly when it comes to interactions and what we choose to engage. It is our power; it energizes that on which we focus and starves that on which we do not.

Chapter 7, The Social Aspects of Choice, focuses on how choice is informed by one's environment and how one participates in collective choice. I highlight what I found most important about Carole Pateman's work on political efficacy. She identifies three social structures that shape political efficacy — family, particularly the form of discipline; schools, and their ability to teach participation; and work that offers opportunities for participation in decision making. She concludes that across all three spheres, participation tends to be limited for the working class and available for the middle class. Further, the results are cumulative, such that high-status people have more opportunities for learning and access to effective participation. I rely on the work of Sherry R. Arnstein to demonstrate how one's ability to effectively participate in society is, in turn, shaped by the levels of decision making in which one is invited to participate as a citizen. Leaders seek to decide the level of decision making; they understand that participation in decision making is power, and the extent to which they want to share power determines the level of decision making they attempt to set. Often, civic protest is aimed at fighting to be part of a higher level of decision making. Finally, Steven Lukes offers a multidimensional view of power at the social level, focused on the extent to which conflict is hidden or articulated. Foucault hinted at this when he wrote "silence and secrecy are a shelter for power."

Finally, chapter 8, Supreme Choice, furthers the thinking on Supreme Power introduced in chapter 5. It concludes the section on choice by asserting that one ultimately has choice over everything one experiences. It highlights the practical uses of choice in the work of William Glasser, who proposed, from many years as a therapist, that unhappiness is essentially caused by an inability to have successful, meaningful interactions. He concludes, much in line with Supreme Power philosophy, that mastery in life is the ability to focus one's attention such that one is able to derive joy from day-to-day experiences. Flow states, those rare occasions when one feels the master of one's fate, considered the optimal state, when one is flying high on joy, the thinking on which has been most developed by Mihaly Csikszentmihalyi, occur not when one is relaxing and things are easy but when one is working at the limits of the self in pursuit of something that is both challenging and meaningful.

By this point in the writing, I'm excited about the themes I thought were important repeating across different fields — the importance of choice, the way others shape our relationship to power or the ability to choose, the importance of knowing how to have successful interactions at the edge of difference as critical to increasing choice.

Decision and Choice
The Efficient Unconscious and the Effort of Intention

6

Decision   The act or process of deciding

Choice   Something that is preferable to others

            The right, power, or opportunity to choose

A point of leverage in interactions is decision making. Its role is prefigured in chapter 1, Effective Interactions, which differentiates between supremacist and liberatory power, defining the latter as the ability to decide for oneself and, very carefully, others or, more broadly, the ability to make decisions that are for the good of all. The ability to make liberatory decisions can be developed; this skill is important to a commitment to freedom. One's life is an ongoing process of making decisions; as such, it is readily available and, with intention and practice, can become a site of choice, of liberation.

The accepted Western theory of decision making is known as *expected utility theory*. It comes from the field of economics, is based on the rational agent model, and focuses on risk and certainty. Its main principles are that humans dislike, and therefore seek to avoid, loss and risk in general, and they like, and therefore seek, certainty — and are willing to pay a premium for it. The insurance industry rests on this behavior.

Recent research on decision making amended the rational agent model by observing actual decision behaviors and coined a new term, *prospect theory*. Prospect theory posits that there are two cognitive systems involved in choice. For the sake of simplicity, they are named System 1 and System 2.

System 1, a hidden and unconscious process characterized by intuition and impulses, functions through association — ideas cascading

one from the other, seeking the coherence of a story. It is integrative, helping one group ideas together by how similar they are and any relationships of time, place, and causality. It monitors both one's mind and the external environment continuously, noticing differences and detecting simple relationships quickly. It makes difficult assessments by using heuristics, or trial and error. It seeks to preserve energy and has shortcuts that provide quick and adequate answers; for example, by replacing the difficult question with an easier question to which one knows the answer, such as when someone answers the question "Which political candidate do you think would be the best in office?" with the answer to the candidate one likes, or trusts, the most, because determining who would be the best is a difficult assessment. One is also guided by one's biases when making difficult decisions. Because humans are biased toward survival, one moves toward opportunities and people one considers friends, and away from threats and those one considers foes.

Decisions based on heuristics and biases are adequate but imperfect. Intention is not necessary. Though these include cognitive, emotional, and physical reactions, very little effort is required. It is efficient. Much of it is based on priming, that is, actions that arise from emotions about which one is unaware, based on memories of past experiences. Indicators of System 1 thinking include the role of memories, facial expressions, quick responses that have an all-at-once quality, in that they occur in concert. Decisions are informed by the past and prepare one for the future.

System 2, characterized by self-control, uses task sets that allow one to overcome habitual responses by following explicit instructions. It **compares and then chooses.** It is what is generally referred to as executive control, under which lies the capacity for conflict resolution. System 2 requires a lot of effort. Researchers found that by observing pupil dilation, they could see which tasks require more effort. The more effort a task requires, the more the pupils dilate. System 2 reacts to stimuli by directing attention, which is energy, to a task, or multiple tasks, that lowers the energy wattage across tasks, showing that energy, while replenishable, is also a limited resource at any one time.

Physical and psychic energy is ultimately glucose, the sugar the body makes from food. When it travels through the blood, it is called blood sugar. In order to function, the body makes glucose from carbohydrates and fat. It processes glucose on a daily basis and requires effort, hence the body's sparing use of it.

One's body activates System 2 only when it is alerted by System 1. However, System 2, which is focused on control, thinks it is in charge of the entire decision-making system and that it knows the reasons for its choices. That means that most of one's judgments are made automatically, by decision and not choice, and one overestimates how much choice one exercises.

Research further revealed two key effects. The lower the skill level for a task, the higher the attention, or energy, required. Conversely, the higher the skill, the lower the energy. Thus, the more skill one has in an area, the less energy one expends. Energy usage is also driven by time pressure. The less time one has to accomplish a task, the more effort one makes striving to accomplish it within the allotted time, and, conversely, the more time one has to complete a task, the less effort it requires.

Research also revealed that decisions are not made in a vacuum. The state before a choice is made, or reference point, is experienced as neutral. A simple experiment demonstrates this principle. Line up three bowls of water, such that the bowl on the left is cold, the one on the right warm, and the one in the middle room temperature. Place one hand in the cold water and the other in the warm. Then place both hands in the room temperature water. The water will feel cold to the hand that was previously in the warm water and warm to the hand that was in the cold water. The state before determines how one judges the current one.

Further, there is a prominence of loss aversion; most people dislike losing more than they like winning. In fact, the identified loss-aversion ratio is two to one, meaning that losing $100 and winning $200 dollars feel about the same to most people.

Finally, there is significant inequality in the distribution of pain, or anxiety, across subjects. A small part of the population does most of the suffering. Research has identified two levers, or means of agency, to one's emotional state. One is the focus of one's attention. In other words, one's emotional state is largely determined by that to which one pays attention. The second is the choices one makes about how one uses time. These two resources — attention and time — are, for the most part, under one's control and key to how much emotional pain one bears.

Though many people use decision making and choice interchangeably to refer to the act of making a judgment, the two do differ. The difference in their definition is tied to the difference between System 1 and System 2. Choice is defined as the act of deciding between two or more possibilities, while the act of decision making is satisfied with thinking only about one option. System 1 supports decision making, and System 2 supports choice.

In chapter 3, Transmission of Affect, freedom is defined as the ability to be free of negative affects, one's own and those of another. This ability rests on one's ability to make choices that disrupt the cycle of negative affect, which itself rests on awareness. Prospect theory reveals that most of one's choices are in fact decisions made outside of awareness. This poses a challenge for intentionality and reflects the difficulty of, the self-effort required for, conscious, powerful living.

While one makes decisions all the time, choice is intentional. It requires attention and effort, two resources the body deploys strategically. However, through intention and practice, one can expand one's awareness, moving more of one's judgments from System 1 to System 2. This is possible because the more skill one develops, the less energy one expends and the more is available for further growth. This is important because the body seeks to preserve energy, so the less energy one needs to make choices, the more one is able to. It is a positive cycle. Increasing this ability enables one to make intentional choices that enact liberatory power.

The Social Aspects of Choice
Participation in Decision Making

7

During a family visit, Luna heard her mother and sister speak about her nephew Primo not doing well in school. They concluded that he was just not very smart. Dismayed, Luna asked them not to speak that way in front of Primo, and proposed that he come live with her for a while so that she could help him catch up in school. Luna knew that research had found that students who were not doing reading and math at level by third grade tended to fall so far behind that it was difficult for them to ever catch up. Her sister agreed. The first few weeks, Luna worked with Primo for hours each day, giving him simple addition and subtraction exercises. Primo sat at the kitchen table with a resigned look on his face, barely trying. Luna encouraged him and cheered each small victory, saying, "You see Primo? You can do it!" This went on for weeks, until one day Primo began to really try and quickly learned his way through increasingly challenging lessons. It was breakthrough for both of them, as Primo gained confidence in himself as a student and Luna realized the extent to which Primo's environment taught him not to have faith in himself as a learner.

Most people live in society. Whether in one's family, at school, at work, or in community, to interact means one's choices intersect with other people's choices and their relative power to realize them. When individual choices interact, it is referred to as decision making. The term does not correlate to whether the decision is one where more than one option is considered, which at the individual level would more accurately be called choice, as explored in chapter 6, Decision and Choice. In fact, at the social level, the use of the term "decision making" spans from covert decision making to specific and explicit processes.

The ability to engage with others in community — whether at the level of neighborhood, city, state, national, or global — is called political efficacy.

Research in political efficacy has found that there are different levels of political efficacy and they are linked to class status, with middle-class people scoring higher than working-class people. These differences are already discernible in working- and middle-class children. Further, there are three core authority structures that shape political efficacy: family, school, and work.

Working-class families tend to have authoritarian discipline structures with inconsistent patterns, while middle-class families tend to have participatory discipline structures that are generally consistent. In this first, and most personal, sphere one learns the extent to which one can shape another's experience. *Luna remembers a time she and her daughter Zoe were at an extended family picnic. Zoe kept trying to run out into the street, and Luna had to watch her vigilantly while she talked to her cousin Nora. Luna would grab her daughter gently as she ran into the street when she thought her mother wasn't looking. Repeatedly, Luna explained that she couldn't run into the street because she could get hurt. At one point, Nora, bewildered, said, "You know, you can just hit your child. She's obviously not listening to you." Luna felt uncomfortable and did not respond. She already knew that her family saw her as different and perhaps even judged her ways uppity. Not demanding obedience from one's child can be seen as irresponsible parenting.*

Schools that serve middle-class children tend to create opportunities for participatory experiences, while those that serve working-class children tend not to. Middle-class children tend to go on to college and increase their opportunities for participatory experiences, while working-class children tend not to. *Luna noticed that while Primo's urban school still made children stand facing a corner when they misbehaved, Zoe's independent school continuously found creative ways to teach their students how to exercise choice. They voted for different activities, offered an engaging curriculum, and focused on rewarding outstanding behavior. For example, one teacher kept a big glass jar with a line marked on it toward the top. Each day the class behaved well, she dropped a jelly bean into the jar. Whenever a student did something outstanding, a jelly bean would also go into the jar. Once the jar of jelly beans reached the line, the class had a party.*

Working-class people tend to work in environments that offer limited participation opportunities, while middle-class people often experience participation opportunities on the job. *Growing up, Luna's mother worked in a garment factory. She remembers the day her mother, who was generally mild mannered, came home ranting because the boss had decided that employees had to punch out their time card when they used the bathroom, and punch back in when they were done. Her mother was insulted by this new policy and refused to go along. "We are people," she said, "not machines!" Here, choice about something as elemental as bathroom use became a site of resistance.*

In all three spheres, participation tends to be limited for the working class and available for the middle class. Participation levels correlate across family, school, and work, and the results are cumulative, such that high-status people have more opportunities for learning, and access to, effective participation.

Though family is a source of origin of one's sense of efficacy, research shows that political efficacy is best learned in two spheres — at work and in local politics. At work, at a minimum, one should have control over one's immediate area of responsibility, meaning one should be able to choose how to best carry out one's work. At the maximum, one should be able to participate in decisions at the organizational level. Employee involvement in decision making is better for the organization because one learns to participate more effectively, one is more committed to collective decisions, and one is more satisfied and willing to contribute the best.

Eventually, business management researchers learned that the tradeoff in decision making is always between involvement and ownership. The higher the level of involvement, the higher the sense of ownership of the decision. The *Levels of Involvement in Decision Making* framework was developed to help leaders navigate this tradeoff.

At the lowest level, *decide and announce,* the leader makes the decision and announces it to the team. The advantage of this approach is speed,

Levels of Involvement in Decision Making

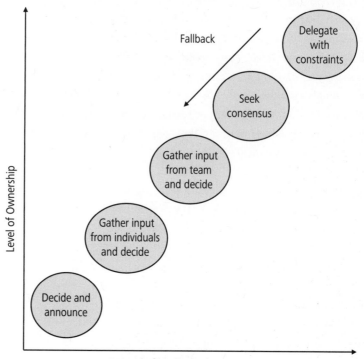

Level of Ownership (vertical axis)

Level of Involvement (horizontal axis)

Circles from bottom to top:
- Decide and announce
- Gather input from individuals and decide
- Gather input from team and decide
- Seek consensus
- Delegate with constraints

Fallback

and the disadvantage is that people may block imposed decisions or the decision may not be the best one because it is based on one person's data and thinking style. One way to mitigate this approach is to share with the team the rationale for using it and the criteria for selection. Sometimes, such as in times of emergency, this is the best level to use because there is not enough time for deliberation. The next level up is *gather input from individuals and decide.* Here, the leader talks to a few individuals, makes the decision, and then announces it to the team. This permits more inclusion and allows for advice that may be useful. However, those consulted may be resentful if they see that their advice has been ignored. Again, this approach can be mitigated by sharing the rationale and criteria and keeping people informed throughout the process.

Further up is *gather input from the team and decide.* The leader gathers input from everyone on the team and then announces the decision to the team. This approach builds shared understanding because everyone is involved. However, like the previous approach, there may be shared resentfulness if the advice is ignored. Even further up is *seek consensus.* This approach most satisfies the principles of collaboration. However, a disadvantage is an inability to reach agreement. This can be mitigated by having a fallback at the outset — an agreement to make a decision at the next lower level of involvement and a period of time within which to make the decision. Finally, the leader can remove himself altogether from the process by using *delegate with constraints.* This allows the leader to focus on other activities, but, again, inability to reach agreement on a decision is a possibility, so a fallback should be declared at the outset.

Work that supports employee decision making helps increase participation in local politics because one is more skilled than one would be otherwise simply because one has more opportunity to practice. Over time, the practice of decision making increases confidence in one's ability to participate in and influence one's government.

In the 1960s, differences between the United States federal government and citizens over participatory processes in planning and programs led to the development of the Ladder of Citizen Participation framework by participatory democracy advocates. The Ladder of Citizen Participation is a typology for civic participation that seeks maximum feasible participation. It explicitly equates citizen participation with citizen power. **Power is participation in decision making.** Further, it proposed that participation is effective if it redistributes power between the haves and the have-nots. Real participation changes the status quo. The framework focused on decision making in three areas: problem definition, resource allocation, and implementation oversight.

Both the Levels of Involvement in Decision Making and the Ladder of Citizen Participation outline levels of power in decision making. This is useful because it allows for clarity about the extent of give and take

LADDER OF CITIZEN PARTICIPATION			
	Level	Description	Example
High	Citizen Control	Citizens have complete decision-making power over policy, governance, and conditions for negotiation	Neighborhood corporations with direct control of resources
	Delegated Power	Citizens have dominant decision making authority	Bargaining is initiated by the power holder in response to the citizens' decision
	Partnership	Negotiation between citizens and power holders	Ground rules cannot be changed unilaterally
	Placation	Ability to influence decision through advice	Tokenism
	Consultation	Inviting opinions	Attitude surveys, neighborhood meetings, public hearings
	Informing	One-way flow of information, no feedback sought	Sharing superficial information and discouraging questions
	Therapy	To cure citizen pathology	Trainings that aim to adjust values
Low	Manipulation	To engineer support	No shared problem definition

and supports open and clear negotiation. However, one framework, the Levels of Involvement in Decision Making, is from the leader's perspective and seeks to balance involvement and ownership. The other framework, the Ladder of Citizen Participation, is from the participant's perspective and seeks to maximize participation. The fact that the Ladder of Citizen Participation explicitly seeks a redistribution of power while the Levels of Involvement specifically notes the need to manage resentment supports the assertion that the relationship between leader and participant, or dominant and subordinate, is constantly negotiated.

Underlying the issue of political efficacy is the way power is defined and deployed in society. The *three-dimensional view* of power framework proposes that the definition of power itself is political and that power acts on at least three dimensions of society. The *one-dimensional view* focuses on overt behavior, specifically decision making, and more specifically conflict. Its actors are citizens. They are part of the system. They participate by articulating policy preferences. The *two-dimensional view* focuses on covert conflict, or the ability to confine the decision-making scope, to effectively prevent conflict articulation. It works through the mobilization of bias — a set of dominant values, beliefs, and institutional procedures that benefit select groups in society. We could say that the Levels of Involvement framework is one-dimensional, as it focuses on explicit decision making, and the Ladder of Citizen Participation is two-dimensional in its attempt to reveal the power dynamics underlying the decision-making process. The *three-dimensional view* of power offers a typology for covert power.

Types of Covert Power

Authority	Command that is recognized
Influence	The ability to cause change without threat
Coercion	The threat of deprivation
Manipulation	The choice is not recognized
Force	The removal of choice

While the two-dimensional view exercises covert power through bias, the three-dimensional view is the space of social arrangements that shape preferences and define reality for most, such that conflict itself is prevented. This is ultimate power, for it is the power to shape desire, such that one cannot help but internalize dominant values and beliefs, and support institutional procedures that favor the dominant. One on whom covert power is exercised is not part of the political system. One is more likely to articulate grievances than policy preferences. One is a resident, not a citizen. One resides in the community, but has no decision-making power. The ideal, or strategic, response is to identify issues, actual and potential — that is, not yet articulated — that challenge the resources of power and authority over policy. This is Gramsci's hegemony, as described in chapter 5, Powerless and Powerful Identities. The ideal response is to identify minoritarian interests — that is, interests that are marginalized, which challenge majoritarian politics, or the politics of the dominant. Women, for example, are usually not a minority, but women's interests are more often than not marginalized in today's prevalence of patriarchal societies. These minoritarian challenges are often based on claiming the benefits of participation on which democracies are founded.

Supreme Choice
Mastery Over Inner Experience

8

When Zoe was two years old, her father Ali came to visit her to say goodbye. It was right after the September 11, 2001, terrorist attacks in the United States, and Ali, an activist exiled in the United States, was once again fleeing, this time to Canada. Zoe saw her father a few times after that, when her mother drove her to Montreal. Soon, however, the distance and the suffering separated them, and Zoe didn't reconnect with her father until she was sixteen years old. It was the night before Zoe was leaving to go to a boarding school for a semester to study ethics and global leadership. Though she now had a wonderful stepfather who had raised her since she was four, Zoe wanted a relationship with the elusive Ali. Her mother always spoke highly of him. She encouraged Zoe to love her father and to not hold his absence against him. She also warned Zoe not to expect too much from him. He had suffered a lot in this life, having been exiled for more than half of his life at that point. Zoe has a close relationship with her father now. He is not always available, but she has learned that his absence is not about her. It is not an indication of her worth. It is the result of his trauma. She is able to love him unconditionally, freely.

The dominant approach in American psychology focuses on external control, or coercion, as a reasonable means to get what one wants. Coercion is, essentially, the punishment of behavior one considers wrong and the rewarding of behavior one judges to be right. Coercion, however, invariably inspires resistance and, ultimately, results in unhappiness for all involved. Luckily, there are alternatives to the external control approach.

According to *choice theory*, **one chooses everything one experiences, including the misery one feels**. It proposes, from practical therapeutic experience, that the major cause of unhappiness stems from the inability to get along with others, particularly those one loves. In other words, **unhappiness is the inability to have successful, meaningful interactions**. Choice theory offers one core question to guide our interactions with others: *Does this action bring me closer to or further apart from this person?*

The sensory input one receives from external stimuli is simply information. It does not determine one's response. Both controlling others and allowing oneself to be controlled are destructive. The developmental goal for one committed to liberation is internal control so that one could make intentional decisions about critical areas of life.

The function of consciousness is to represent internal and external information in a way that helps one identify decisions and desires. Consciousness bridges experiences and goals. However, consciousness is limited by one's nervous system's ability to process information. The information that makes it into one's consciousness is a small fraction of the information that is available in any given situation. One forms goals in order to prioritize internal and external information. At any point in life, one's current self is a representation of one's goals.

Anxiety occurs when one is aware of information that conflicts with one's goals. Information can either reinforce one's goals, which frees up psychic energy, or conflict with one's goals, which uses up psychic energy. For example, a student wants to earn a college degree, but her single-parent mother is not supportive and is pushing her to move into her own apartment. The student feels unsupported and insufficiently loved. She finds she has to work to stay motivated to achieve her goals. The accumulation of this kind of information may eventually lead to a weakening of one's ability to invest attention in the pursuit of one's goals. The more energy one uses to relieve anxiety, the less there is for creativity and joy.

However, in the world of events, information has no positive or negative value. One attaches value to information by the way one experiences and makes meaning of it. To follow the example above, the student can note that her mother is not supportive of her goal to earn a college degree and spend her energy resisting this reality by refusing to move out and waging an ongoing battle with her mother for not being supportive. She can also realize that, though her mother struggles to be supportive, she herself works and earns a moderate income and might be better off living with roommates who are supportive. She can set a goal to create a supportive living condition beyond her relationship with her mother.

Control over the content of one's consciousness is key to controlling the inner experience, but it requires great effort. It relies on one's mind's ability to filter experiences, such that one crafts quality experiences from the events in life. As these quality experiences accumulate, one becomes more complex and refines the ability to choose. Similarly, the root of discontent is internal. One's inability to push beyond one's current limit to meet a challenge causes anxiety.

Mastery is the ability to focus one's attention such that one is able to derive joy from day-to-day experiences. Optimal experience, the rare occasion when one feels the master of one's fate, is called *flow*. There are key conditions that enable flow states. The first is that, contrary to contemporary belief, optimal states occur not when one is making little effort but when one is working at limits of the self, that is, when one is stretched beyond current capacity, while in the pursuit of something that is challenging and meaningful. *Challenging* is defined as having skills that are adequate, a task slightly beyond one's reach, and a feedback loop that lets one know how one is doing against clear rules or guide posts. Challenges are meaningful when the endeavor is in the pursuit of one's goals. The cumulative effect of experiences in which one meets and overcomes a challenge is mastery in the ability to determine the content of one's life, how one shapes, as well is shaped by, experiences.

Another key condition of flow is ordered consciousness, the ability to detect meaningful patterns in one's experiences. When an experience is slightly beyond one's current skill level, one must focus all of one's attention, or psychic energy, to perceive a solution, often at the level of pattern recognition, the matching of new data with information retrieved from memory. There is no excess energy available for anxiety. To focus one's attention this way at will is to be in control of one's consciousness. Ordering consciousness allows increasing control over one's feelings and thoughts, inner experience, quality of life. Personalities are patterns for structuring attention. There are countless daily opportunities to expand one's self, beyond one's current personality. The ordering of one's experiences becomes the ordering and reordering of personality.

Key Flow Conditions

Working at one's limit	Challenging and meaningful pursuits
Ordered consciousness	Ability to detect patterns; ability to focus one's attention

Just as there are conditions that contribute to flow, there are conditions that inhibit flow. *Oppression* can be described as the elimination of enjoyment. People who endure oppression have to work harder to find enjoyment in life. When one oppresses people, one steals their joy. *Anomie* is a social condition in which the rules or norms are unclear; one does not understand how things work, so one cannot set goals toward which to work. This is the case with people who are uprooted, such as refugees. *Alienation* is a condition in which one knows what one's goals are but cannot reach them. One turns one's attention away from one's goals and does not seek their fulfillment. There are also personal traits that inhibit flow. One's attention can be too fluid, such as with *attentional disorder*; or it can be too rigid, as with *self-centeredness*.

Key Flow Inhibitors

Oppression	The elimination of joy
Anomie	Lack of clear rules or norms
Alienation	Social conditions inhibit one's goals
Attentional disorder	The inability to focus one's attention
Self-centeredness	A tendency toward rigidity

Activities that promote flow are pleasurable. Pleasurable activities are referred to as games. Their function is to help transcend current experience. There are four types of games: competition, chance, consciousness altering, and creation of alternative realities.

In competition, the challenge is one's opponent. Examples are sports and board games. In chance, the challenge is to control the future, such as with bingo and dice. In consciousness altering games, the challenge is to alter one's consciousness. This includes merry-go-rounds, skydiving, and roller-coasters. In games that allow the creation of alternative realities, such as theater, the challenge is to be more than one currently is.

Flow is about paying attention to one's internal and external environments and identifying ways to advance toward one's goals. In flow, one's goals are realizable, if not promised. One is able to track progress, reach goals, and set bigger ones. Over time, one evolves into an increasingly complex and thoughtful being. As a master, one would be able to control one's consciousness, no matter what the environment.

Power + Thresholds

Creating the Self

Power + Thresholds Intro
Rites of Passage

Is there a particular space where the fine-tuning of consciousness overlaps with the transformation from one level of consciousness to another? If there is, what does it look like and how does one move through it?

Chapter 9, Rites of Passage, highlights Victor Turner's thinking on liminality, the space of transformation, the ritual of transitioning from one state to another. One leaves behind previous identities, practices, and routines to make room for a more expansive set. Rites of passage begin with a threshold — a challenge one cannot meet without transcending one's current idea of oneself. They show up differently in simple and complex societies. In simple societies, rites of passage show up as rituals that function to compensate for the unfairness in the system, as all systems are simply current stable states of power, or status quo, inherent in which is difference or conflict. In complex societies, difference and conflict show up as antistructure, or social critiques of injustice and leisure, or entertainment. In both simple and complex societies, the social role of rites of passage or liminality is to relieve the anxiety of differences in status.

Theater as Interaction and Identity Creation, chapter 10, explores the first of two social spaces that at their core are about the exchange of power — theater and games. Fundamentally, to act is to accept difference enough to engage in dialogue with another. Central to exchanges of power, particularly where there is perceived difference, is status. Improvisational theater — a form of live theater in which the plot, characters, and dialogue of a scene are made up in the moment — turns on understanding how to read, play, and shift status, which always drives the story forward. While Turner identified the social dramas of everyday life as the microtheater of differences in status, Keith Johnstone, the leading thinker on the central role of status in masterful acting, asserted that the microinteractions of everyday life are the essence of both power and theater. For Johnstone, a status expert is not someone who can enact dominance most of the time, but someone who can play a range of statuses and can raise or lower status at will to best cope with external situations. Johnstone used status games to help actors understand the language of status and learn how to choose status at will.

I was excited to discover, through the research for this book, that there are frameworks and practices in the world of theater that allow one to engage power shifting in an embodied way. As a social-change practitioner, I saw that much of this transformation process occurs at the intellectual level, or in the head. It is often full of judgment and self-righteousness. I believe there is a strong need to balance this with body, spirit, and heart. These acting frameworks and practices are one way out of replicating dominant power in spaces devoted to freedom and liberation.

Rites of Passage
Self-formation in Liminal Space

9

S asha felt a strong movement of energy in her body expanding and push-ing outward. She saw images of metal armor and realized she had built it, below her awareness, over the years. Her head throbbed. She retched. The armor was cracking and expelling stuck energy with an outward-bound force. She realized that, though it had served her well, she didn't need the armor anymore. It was getting in the way now. She was strong. She could feel that the new path is about connecting and flowing, not protecting or fighting.

A threshold occurs when one is presented with a challenge one can-not meet without transcending one's current idea of oneself. These moments occur throughout life, inviting one into larger, more complex states of being. One begins to notice that an approach that has worked in getting one's needs and wants met no longer works as well. Or one becomes bored with one's own story, its limitations. It no longer moti-vates. Rites of passage are the way societies have, for millennia, allowed people to consciously transcend from a no-longer-useful state to an as-yet-defined one.

Rites of passage mark a transition between two states. They have three phases: separation, liminality, and incorporation. Separation is charac-terized by symbolic behavior that signifies detachment from the earlier state, a fixed point in a social structure. **One leaves behind previous identities, practices, and routines.**

States are stable, recurring, culturally recognized conditions. Their work is to structure what is normative, the current working equilibrium, or status quo. They are defined by structure, and are cognitive, abstract, and secular in nature. Their products are political, legal, and familial. Examples are offices, roles, rights, and obligations, such as wife, mayor, child. States foster heterogeneity, a focus on difference and status, which gives rise to conflict. They are marked by the avoidance of pain and suffering.

Liminality, the core phase of rites of passage, is characterized by ambiguity. It is unstructured space where one can reformulate elements of the old state into a new pattern. One is no longer in a past state and not yet in a future one. As a result, one is invisible — no longer and not yet classified, not easily understood by others. The experience is void of status yet full of possibility. The change is not just in knowledge or role but in being. What occurs is an expansion, an absorption of power that becomes manifest in the final, incorporation, phase.

From a social perspective, liminal space is dangerous. Because it lies outside of the status quo, the classification systems that orders society, it can challenge the structures of society. However, it is also the potential that arises in response to crises to become the source of new culture.

Further, liminality is about play, as opposed to the work of states. The recombination of familiar elements from the previous, now-deconstructed, structure into new forms, though rigorous, is also playful. Play figures prominently in the world of mythology. In Indian mythology, for example, the world is a play of consciousness. Play is also a site of suppression. For example, the Protestant Ethic, which is the foundation of American Christianity, was ardently anti-play, ushering in a new culture that supported the rise of capitalism. Key features were the minimization of ritual, or sacred work, and the rise of the profane work of capitalism — working hard for the sake of work, working hard as a virtue. Play was the enemy of work. The Protestant Ethic gathered the energy of society and directed it toward mass production for profit. It suppressed Shakti, the playful creative force of the Universe, in all her forms, including Mary (Protestants do not worship Mary, as the Catholics do) and the "witches" of Salem.

To delve into liminality is to explore ritual, or formalized rites of passage. While informal rituals occur in modern society, formal rituals are largely found in premodern societies. These rituals have social, personal, and sacred dimensions. In ritual space, the social model of interrelatedness is of undifferentiated community. This invokes an evolutionary life force akin to the Shiva Consciousness of ancient India outlined in chapter 5, Powerful and Powerless Identities, which connects one to the Supreme Power that is above and beyond current material manifestation. There are two major relationship types in ritual. The first is one's relationship to the master guide, or guru. The master guide has complete authority and represents the absolute values of and for the common good. Relationships with peers, others undergoing the same ritual at the same time, are characterized by egalitarianism. In unstructured space, there are no ranks or roles. Interactions are immediate and concrete. There is integrity in one's ability and opportunity to be one's true self. These relationships tend to be characterized by an enduring and far-reaching hospitality. In addition to community, the social products of liminal space are art and spirituality. Artists and prophets are ambiguous beings that tend to question their culture's social classification.

One's behavior in ritual is passive — subject to larger community values, norms, and relationship to the whole of existence. One explores silence, obeys the instructions of the guide, and is willing to accept pain and suffering. Practicing restraint builds the ability to refrain from advancing one's personal interests and abusing any new powers. For example, in premodern societies, one who is in ritual to attain chiefdom may be subject to community members' grievances and remonstrations to create an experience of and instill a sense of servanthood in a future leadership state.

In ritual, one is closer to deities, can tap into superhuman power, and can experience unbounded and limitless reality. One simultaneously experiences the power of the Universe and the power of the weak. There is sacredness in having a low position. The power of the lowly positioned is the power of universal values.

In ritual, or liminal space, one experiences speech as creative power. One sees how words create reality. As outlined in chapter 5, Powerless and Powerful Identities, the masters of consciousness understand the power of speech, which is Matrika Shakti, as that which brings forth physical reality. Speech is central to the process of self-formation. Our internal stories manifest external realities.

The sacred dimension of ritual is made up of exhibitions, instructions, and actions. Exhibitions are what is shown, what represents the invisible and unknown. This includes deities, masks, musical instruments, and medicine or plants. These help shift consciousness, allowing one to experience a larger identity. They provide an experience of the identity into which one is moving. While exhibitions are simple, their interpretations are complex. They reveal the powers that underlie reality, how the human body is a microcosm of the Universe, that what is sacrosanct — the ultimate mystery — is beyond rational processes.

Instructions, what is said in ritual, are revelations of what is real and secret. They are the outlines of cosmogony, a theory of Universal origin and evolution. Sacred chants that awaken the experience of oneness are also instructions.

Finally, actions are what is done that allows one to see what was previously accepted unthinkingly, one's social conditioning. The reduction of culture into recognizable components builds understanding of the social forces that drive one and open up the space for redirection. Actions also include the recombination of patterns of past states. These recombinations are brought forward into the next, new state.

In the final phase of rites of passage, incorporation, one consummates the passage. One is stable once again. A new status has been achieved. The new status may be a social role or an evolution in consciousness. The integration of new and disturbing experiences has brought one to a new state. There is a return to the world of social structures, with its concomitant rights and obligations. This is the beginning of a new phase of life where one is learning to integrate the experiences of liminality into the new, as yet unmanifested, state. As one returns to everyday reality, one seeks to remember the experience of connection to a larger reality. While undergoing the trials of liminality, one may have looked forward to the next phase of stability and relative comfort. However, in liminality one is in an expanded state, and stability brings the contraction required to live in structured, social reality. This paradox of expansion-discomfort/contraction-stability is held until one fully transitions into the next phase and the liminal experience is a faint whisper, integrated into ongoing existence — until the next disruption. Incorporation is a dialectic, a juxtaposition of the opposing forces of the concrete and immediate community of liminality and the abstract and impersonal structures of society.

Rites of passage show up differently in simple and complex societies. The formal aspects of ritual described above occur in simple societies, such as tribal societies. Societies are simple when members have shared values. Simple societies are stable, cyclical, and repetitive, and the symbols of their liminal space reflect this. Relationships adhere to status. Ritual is obligatory in the sense that it is communal. One does not have the choice to not participate because it is happening all around. One is anonymous in it, one of the many people undergoing it, enveloped by it. The choice to participate is unnecessary. **In simple societies, rites of passage, or liminal spaces, show up as rituals that function to compensate for the unfairness in the system.** They are collective, a space where people can interact outside of status roles. The feeling is of work, effort. It is sacred work where one has a choice to make about how to move beyond the current, now limiting, state. There are four options:

1. Conform to status, roles, and expectations for which the ritual is a vehicle
2. Perceive the underlying latent nonconformity as one adheres to status, roles, and expectations
3. Get lost in the chaos of disorder
4. Transform to a higher consciousness (such as those described in chapter 5, Powerless and Powerful Identities)

Societies in which people have different values, such as industrial societies, are complex. Relationships are reciprocal and contractual, a network of varying and shifting power dynamics. **In complex societies, difference and conflict show up as antistructure — social critiques of injustices.** It is a personal choice to participate, and participation is individual. One may choose liminality as a way to reject dominant social values and work with others to actively create alternatives. Liminality also lives outside the world of work, **in the shrinking space of play known as leisure time.** It is social movements, the narrative worlds of theater and film, and spiritual communities. **In both simple and complex societies, the social role of rites of passage, or liminality, is to relieve the anxiety of differences in status.** Liminality, then, is a space for coming to terms with and assuaging society's value structures, which are based on difference, to connect to the larger reality that connects us all.

10

Theater as Interaction and Identity Creation
High-status and Low-status Characters

Social change agents tend to focus on systemic change, or fighting the social structures of domination. However, structures are the artifacts of interactions. A deeper lever for change is at the level of interactions. This may seem small, unimportant, or abstract, but it is essentially a shift at the level of being. The state of being of the social change agent is the most powerful force for change. One can fight for freedom, or one can enact freedom.

Theater offers useful frameworks and practices for enacting power through its focus on reflecting, or representing, the interactions that shape individuals in society. Theater Status Games, Audition Sign Posts, and Theater of the Oppressed are examples of theater frameworks and practices that help the social-change agent shift power at the level of interactions. **At its core, theater is about the exchange of power**.

In *Waiting for Godot*, a play about status, there are four characters. Vladimir and Estragon are lifelong friends. Vladimir believes himself to be superior, but Estragon does not accept this positioning. They are peers who, through friendship, shift status back and forth. They have a minimum status gap. Pozzo and Lucky have a master/slave relationship, the maximum status gap. Vladimir and Estragon intently observe the interactions of Pozzo and Lucky. Pozzo yells commands, and Lucky obeys, unless ordered to disobey. Estragon asks Pozzo why Lucky holds his bags instead of resting them on the ground.

Pozzo: Ah! Why couldn't you say so before? Why he doesn't
            make himself comfortable? Let's try and get this clear.
            Has he not the right to? Certainly he has. It follows that

	he doesn't want to. There's reasoning for you. And why doesn't he want to? [Pause.] Gentlemen, the reason is this.
Vladimir:	[To Estragon]: Make a note of this.
Pozzo:	He wants to impress me, so that I'll keep him.
Estragon:	What?
Pozzo:	Perhaps I haven't got it quite right. He wants to mollify me, so that I'll give up the idea of parting with him. No, that's not exactly it either.
Vladimir:	You want to get rid of him?
Pozzo:	He wants to cod me, but he won't.
Vladimir:	You want to get rid of him?
Pozzo:	He imagines that when I see him indefatigable I'll regret my decision. Such is his miserable scheme. As though I were short of slaves! [All three look at Lucky.] Atlas, son of Jupiter! [Silence.] Well, that's that I think. Anything else?
Vladimir:	You want to get rid of him?
Pozzo:	Remark that I might just as well have been in his shoes and he in mine. If chance had not willed otherwise. To each one his due.

Social animals tend to create rules for interactions designed to establish norms for distributing opportunities and resources, such as food, mates, and the ability to offload one's anxiety onto others. As quickly as one is trained to understand and cooperate with these, one is encouraged to ignore them and to believe that one's actions are without power purposes.

In theater, **to act is to accept difference enough to engage in dialogue with another.** When one acts across difference, it often produces a reaction. Some of those reactions are about conflict. These are deconstructed and reflected in stage theater, which is society's metacommentary.

In everyday life, everyone is an actor. The microstructure of theater is everyday social dramas — spontaneous, unauthorized conflict events. They reveal society's classification of relationships — kinship ties, structural positions, social class, and political status. Social dramas are the discrete, microinteractions of everyday life in which there is conflict and choice. One's action either supports or disrupts status relations, contracts or expands consciousness.

Social dramas have four phases. They begin with a breach of a norm, which is experienced as a political act that challenges the power structure. This activates oppositions, the awareness of class interests. In the next phase, crisis, group members take positions, siding with either the rule breaker or the target of the rule breaker's action. Next, group members responsible for the continuity of structure and the dispelling of crises that threaten it — parents, chiefs, elders, legal professionals, priests — attempt redress. The conflict centers on conserving the norm or reforming it. The last phase is restoration of peace through reconciliation or mutual acceptance of schism. Restoration of peace is not guaranteed, however, and sometimes social dramas are settled by force, reflecting ideologies that are totalistic, or in opposition to difference.

The microinteractions of everyday life are the essence of both power and theater. These power interactions are dances of potentiality. They are driven by the playing out and reversal of status, one's social position in relation to others. Status is implied in every movement, in every inflection. There is no way to be neutral. Status is something one does, or enacts. One is taught to not see it except when there is explicit conflict. Vladimir and Estragon do not seem to explicitly note their power dynamics the way they can the dynamics between Pozzo and Lucky, which are explicit.

At its essence, status can be distinguished as high and low, with high status being dominant and low status subordinate. Further, there are two different types of status. Social status is assigned by society, and personal status is the status one plays out or enacts. High status inspires high levels of obedience from others, and low status compels low levels.

The core principle of status interactions is the *seesaw principle*. In a dominant interaction, when one person goes up, the other goes down.

However, one may be assigned a low status but play high status. There is an art to doing this successfully, because people generally do not like people who play above their status. **A status expert is someone who can raise and lower their status at will to best cope with external situations.**

At the social level, artist is a high-status role. Artists reflect society's choices and structures and sometimes challenge them. Further, status orders art. For example, tragedies are a product of an actor who acts high status in spite of low-status circumstances. They inspire pleasure in the rising of status. Comedies are stories in which an actor is an expert at lowering his, or another's, status.

People have preferences when it comes to enacting status; that is, people have a preferred status. People who play high status send the message, "Don't mess with me!" Low-status people say, "I'm not worth messing with." One's preferred status is the way one has best learned, to date, to maneuver into the situations that one feels provide advantage.

In contrast, the status expert is undefended and can choose strategically between high and low status. Friends are people who agree to play status games together. There is an ease about sharing high and low status across time. In acting, and in life, knowing which status one is playing may be more important than the words one says.

Status games are a great way to learn how to understand the status one plays and how to choose. Status games come from the world of theater. They help improve interactions by making status explicit, outlining power transactions, and allowing the actor to choose direction.

Theater status games enlist all five senses. As sensory experiences, they serve as rehearsal for future potential life situations. There are talking status games and body-language status games. A simple talking status game is *SeeSaw Talking*, in which two people take turns saying one sentence that raises their own status and lowers the other. In each alternate sentence, they switch to lowering themselves and raising the other. This helps one learn how status exchanges happen, which is necessary because most people are taught to see status interactions as not on purpose, or innocent of power goals.

Another is *Hello*. In this one, the facilitator asks a group to walk around saying "Hello" to each other. It is usually awkward. It doesn't feel real because people don't know what status they should be playing. The group then does a second round with half the group holding initial eye contact and the other breaking initial eye contact and glancing back for a moment. Holding eye contact is powerful, while breaking eye contact and looking back is powerless. Breaking contact and not looking back, however, is powerful.

In *Er*, participants experiment with interrupting their sentences with "Er..." People who say a short "Er..." at the beginning of their sentences are perceived as weaker, as if they are unsure of what they are saying and are inviting people to interrupt them. Those that say a longer "er..." in the middle of their sentences, however, are perceived as confident and important, as expecting people to wait for them to get their thoughts together.

TALKING STATUS GAMES

SeeSaw Talking	Two people take turns saying one sentence that raises their own status and lowers the other's
Hello	A group of people walk around saying, "Hello," to each other; half the group holds eye contact, and the other breaks eye contact and glances back for a moment
Er	Participants experiment with interrupting their sentences with "Er..." Short "Er" at the beginning of a sentence makes one feel weaker. Long "er" in the middle evokes confidence.

Body-language status games bring attention to how we emit power or powerlessness with our bodies. Every movement modifies the space between people. One can take on low-status or high-status body language to evoke the desired status.

The aforementioned *Hello* game includes the body language of *Eye Contact.* In *Posturing,* there are three postures that suggest status. Holding one's head still while talking is perceived as high status, while moving one's head while talking suggests low status. Exposing one's belly reflects dominance and high status, and protecting it connotes fear and low status. Toes pointing inward is low status, while sitting back and spreading legs apart is high status. Overall, a relaxed posture corresponds to high status, indicating one feels secure. Anxiety reflects low status. Chapter 3, Transmission of Affect, highlights excess anxiety as a sign of low status that results from being compelled to upload the anxiety of the offloading dominant.

One's *Movements* express status. Smooth body movements indicate high status, while jerky body movements denote low status. Putting one's hands near one's face while speaking is low status; hands away from face while talking is high status. Moving slowly is high status, and moving fast is low status.

Finally, how one relates to *Space* reveals status. Dominant people act as if the space belongs to them, while subordinate people act as if the space belongs to other, more dominant, people. High-status people allow their space to flow into the space of others. Low-status people avoid having their space flow into the space of others. One can learn to be conscious both of not taking up too much space and taking up appropriate space.

Most interactions break down into either blocking or accepting. Blocking and accepting are central in improvisational theater. A block is anything that prevents action from developing. Blocking is a form of control, a form of aggression. However, it is also a way of seeking safety. An acceptance is a response that helps develop action. High-status people are more likely to block, and low-status people more likely to accept. To engage in relationship, one moves toward acceptance.

BODY-LANGUAGE GAMES		
Area	HI Status Dominant	LO Status Subordinate
Eye Contact	Staring	Looking away
	Looking away	looking back
Posturing	Hold head still while talking	Move head while talking
	Expose belly	Protect belly
	Legs spread apart	Toes pointing inwards
	Relaxed	Anxious
Movements	Smooth	Jerky
	Hands away from face while talking	Hands near face while talking
	Slow	Fast
Space	Belongs to them	Cedes to others
	Flow into others	Avoid flowing into others

Good improvisational actors are able to accept and develop action. An improvisational scene, much like the microinteractions of everyday life, generates spontaneously if both actors both make and accept offers. It is a generative cycle. Once a group understands the key characteristics of status, it can play four kinds of status scenes.

KEY STATUS SCENES

- Both lower status
- Both raise status
- One raises while the other lowers
- Status is reversed

Status is so important to understanding identity that it is considered a key factor in auditions. In an audition, an actor has to become someone different quickly and does not have time to learn the character. The actor has to identify the relevant information that allows interaction effective enough to land the role. An audition is akin to a spontaneous interaction, in that there is not much history and an exchange will take place.

Luckily, masters of auditions have left behind audition guideposts to help the actor, on the stage and in everyday life. The first is *Relationship — What is one's emotional attitude toward the other*? This is not about the social role one plays out with the other but the feeling one has about the other. It is not just that he is her husband but that she considers him her best friend. Which is very different from her regretting having married him. Audition masters recommend actors seek maximum relationship, or maximum engagement, because it is the most interesting.

The second audition guidepost is *Conflict — What is each actor fighting for*? In interactions across difference and conflict, there is something that makes the actors stay in the relationship. That is what they are fighting for. She may remember a time when she was his world... and yearns to make him love her like that again. She may want her father's approval but acts as if he does not matter. The conflict is the drama, the story.

The third guidepost is *Discovery — What is new*? This may be about oneself, the other, or the situation. In auditions, the actor is looking for what is not written in the script, the dynamic that will make the interaction come alive. The actor looking for the maximum seeks the possibility of love.

The fourth is *Events — What are the key symbolic interactions*? Events are interactions that change the relationship. They are power interactions. What is important to each actor? Is one winning and the other losing? What feelings sent and received? This is affect. See chapter 3, Transmission of Affect.

AUDITION SIGN POSTS	
Factor	**Question to Answer**
Relationship	What is the character's emotional attitude toward the other characters?
Conflict	What is each actor fighting for?
Discovery	What is new?
Events	What are the key, symbolic interactions?

The *Theater of the Oppressed* approach focuses on interactions of domination to help the subject actor understand and order, or reorder, the experience. There are at least three forms of theater in this approach: forum, image, and ideal image.

In *Forum Theater*, the actor chooses a theme and creates a short scenario between an oppressed and an oppressor. The actor is reexperiencing a challenging interaction and practicing for a different future outcome. Spectators observe, engage in discussion with the actor on the power interaction, and sometimes step in and enact a different strategy for taking power that provides a different, more powerful, outcome for the actor.

In *Image Theater*, the focus is the creation of an image. Words are not necessary; the power relationship is expressed visually. It is group theater in which the group selects the theme, and, without talking, each person positions in relationship to the others in the group and the theme. This creates a mirror effect because the scene is perceived through the gaze of multiple actors. It focuses on the message between senders and receivers, and often reveals the hidden aspects of power relationships, such as the many manifestations of resistance.

Ideal Image Theater reflects the ways oppressors coax submission though repression and seduction. Power, in addition to demanding, seduces — the oppressed take on the desires of the oppressor. In Ideal Image Theater, the focus is on the actor's point of crisis, the moment in the relationship when different alternatives are possible. The actor relives an unsuccessful life scene to reimagine it in a more idealized form. It is like the practice of reconstruction in patterns of resistance, in chapter 2, Interaction Patterns.

At its core, the Theater of the Oppressed approach is about the power of aesthetic images, whether moving or still, spoken or silent. It does not seek convergence, or agreement. It asserts that images of power in interactions are transformative because they can reorder past aggressions and ready the actor, and vicariously the spectator, for future similar power interactions. These images tap into, explore, amplify, and redirect sensory knowledge. It is a cathartic experience, a ritual that transforms anxiety into joy and freedom.

THEATER OF THE OPPRESSED

• Forum Theater	Short scenarios of domination explore what could be done differently to shift power dynamics
• Image Theater	Visual images of a power interaction
• Ideal Image Theater	A short scene that explores the point of crisis, the moment at which different alternatives become possible and allow a shift in power dynamics

Section Four

Power + Games

Playing with Power

Power + Games Intro
Playing with Power

What is the purpose of games, particularly in relation to power and status? What aspects of games are important? How do they relate to the patterns of resistance outlined in chapter 2, Interaction Patterns?

Chapter 11, The Purpose of Play, begins with Stuart Brown's discovery of the evolutionary purpose of play. Brown outlines the features of play, one being the creation of potential future events that allow one to practice at one's edge and preadapt, or fine-tune one's consciousness a priori. Another feature of play is the engaging of difference. His conclusive definition of play is: a state of mind composed of pleasure, creativity, and innovation; a tuning in to others in the pursuit of something meaningful. Brown also found that people have play personalities, or a preference for certain types of play, and proposes that there are at least eight. Thomas S. Henricks further identified play as one of the four pathways for experience, along with work, communitas, and ritual. Within play, he describes four patterns of self-location, or how one positions oneself vis-à-vis others: privilege, subordination, marginality, and engagement.

Chapter 12, The Structure of Games, delves into the function of games, which is, according to Henricks, to order and reorder interactions with others. It looks at how status impacts the types of games people play and orders interaction patterns between players. Finally, E.M. Avedon provides a summary of the structural elements of games, or the factors to consider in exploring the way power is ordered in games.

Chapters 13 through 24 offer 12 power games that provide practice for the patterns of resistance outlined in chapter 2, Interaction Patterns: sign reading, deconstruction, and reconstruction.

During the process of finishing this book, I had a vision in which my spiritual teacher showed me the Earth. It was off balance. She told me my work was to help rebalance Earth. Overwhelmed with the idea that I could fulfill such a mission, I asked her how I would do this. She responded, "through play." At the time, I wondered how something as small as play could be up to such a task. I set out to explore play and games and am beginning to understand how this could occur.

The Purpose of Play

Play as Evolution

11

What?

Play, or recreational activity, abounds in nature. The more developed the species, the more it seems to play. Play researchers have observed animals choose play over food and wondered, Why would a living being choose something seemingly extraneous, like play, over something necessary for survival, such as food? Does play have a purpose?

Before exploring the purpose of play, it helps to clarify *what* play is. This is not simple. One person's play may be another person's oppression, literally and metaphorically. Play researchers have, however, managed to identify what appear to be features of play.

Pleasure is a feature of play. Play is fun. It energizes. Play takes one to the edge of body and mind. Play heightens the senses and alerts the mind for the unexpected, body pumping, ready for action. Yet play is also calming because it is relatively safe space for engaging the unexpected, since the outcome does not generally have serious consequences. "It is just a game," after all. This engaged, calm excitement is pleasurable.

Another feature of play is that it catalyzes creativity and innovation. Play allows experimentation with different potential realities. Through play, one creates and experiences potential future events and preadapts; that is, one practices and fine-tunes one's response a priori, before the event. Even daydreaming leaves an imprint on the brain. Innovation can be dangerous. One might fail and lose status or, worse, one's life. Trying things out first in play space increases the chances of successful innovation in the structured space of everyday life.

Further, play is about tuning in to the environment and others and engaging difference. Through play, one learns to decipher the intentions of others, for one must anticipate the other in play, either to protect one's move, reduce the options of the other, or support the other in building something together. This act of moving toward the other reduces conflict. It sharpens understanding of fairness and rearranges relationships because it requires sensitivity to the other. As such, play is mutual delight, for this challenge, or support, of the other must be enough to keep the other engaged, because the fourth and final feature of play is that it is always chosen, never imposed. Play's reward is poise — spontaneity, grace, and fulfillment.

Ultimately, play is a state of mind, not simply an activity. Its correlating mind state is flow, considered the optimal state of mind. Optimal states occur not when one is making little effort but when one is working at the limits of the self, that is, when one is stretched beyond current capacity, while in the pursuit of something that is challenging and meaningful. Challenging is defined as having skills that are adequate, a task slightly beyond one's reach, and a feedback loop that lets one know how one is doing against clear rules or guide posts. Challenges are meaningful when the endeavor is in the pursuit of one's goals. The cumulative effect of experiences in which one meets and overcomes a challenge is mastery in the ability to determine the content of one's life, how one shapes, as well is shaped by, experiences.

Thus, **play is a state of mind composed of pleasure, creativity, and innovation, a tuning in to others and the external environment, and choice in pursuit of something meaningful and challenging.**

Why?

What is the purpose? More specifically, why is the play mind state important in the life of human beings?

Emotions figure prominently in considering mind states, or states of mind. An emotion is a mental state that arises spontaneously and is accompanied by physiological changes. Emotions connect the body and the mind. Examples of emotions are joy, sorrow, fear, hate, and love.

Despite the range of emotions available to human beings, one generally toggles back and forth between two key emotional states, anxiety and joy, seeking to minimize anxiety and maximize joy. An interaction that triggers anxiety, a threat response, is emotionally overwhelming and mentally taxing. Anxiety de-energizes. It lowers personal productivity because it diverts and uses up oxygen and glucose, which would otherwise go toward other, more creative, uses. Offloading anxiety increases the likelihood of joy for the offloader. Because play energizes, it increases joy, which helps stabilize body and mood. When play is absent, the mood darkens, one's sense of hope diminishes, and pleasure is unsustainable. Play supports well-being.

Because play supports experimentation and learning it quickens growth and evolution. Because it allows encountering new situations where one can imagine and experience the future and create possibilities, play allows the practice of skills that help create one's future self. Play also preserves the best of past social selves. It sculpts the brain and guides adaptation.

Finally, because play helps human beings learn to move through the environment and the rules of engagement with others necessary in social groups, it helps one learn a public self. It helps one learn the rules of engagement that help differentiate between friend and foe. It is a penalty-free space for rehearsing the social give and take of living in community. Play increases the sense of belonging.

In this way, **play is central to well-being, adaptation, and social cohesiveness.**

How?

How do we play? Given the description of what play is and its purpose, the process of play must support adaptive variability, self-organization, and mutuality.

Play researchers have identified six elements of play. The first is *anticipation*. There has to be the disposition to play; that is, play is something that is chosen. It is never coerced. At its core, play requires choice and free will.

Surprise is also an element of play. Play allows one to break through habitual responses. This supports the emergence of new ideas and ways of being.

Pleasure not only is a feature of play, as mentioned, it is an essential element. If it is not fun, people will not engage, will not choose to play. So play requires fun, which is generative, life-giving. Play increases joy.

Play builds *understanding.* Tuning in to others in an atmosphere of low risk and fun can deliver emotional empathy. One can imagine what it is like to walk in someone else's shoes. This often leads to intellectual insights. One begins to see how another makes sense of the world, and one takes that into account in learning to live together better.

Play also helps build *strength*. It trains physical skills, sharpens mental abilities, deepens social insights and capabilities, and builds mastery and control. As such, play builds strength of body, mind, social interactions, and self.

Finally, play eventually leads to *poise*, the state of balance. Through ongoing, thoughtful, successful engagement with the external world, one builds confidence and self-possession, the ability to determine as much as possible for oneself in light of the fact that one shares the world with others. This disposition helps one move through the world with ease and allows one to direct one's life energy toward growth, expansion, and evolution.

THE KEY ELEMENTS OF PLAY

1.	Anticipation	The disposition, or choice, to play
2.	Surprise	Breaking through habitual responses to new ideas and ways of being

3.	Pleasure	The generative power of fun
4.	Understanding	Seeing how another makes sense of the world
5.	Strength	Building the capacity of body, mind, social interactions, and self
6.	Poise	A state of balance, ease, and optimal use of life energy

Play is a source of power and grace, and this shows up in different ways. Play researchers have found that people have play personalities, that is, a preference for certain types of play over others, usually formed in childhood. There are at least eight play personalities.

The *joker* is the quintessential player, showing up in archetypes, folktales, myths, and religions across the world. In Jungian psychology, it is the jester who uses humor to reflect the paradoxes and hypocrisies of life. In African and Caribbean folktales, it is Anansi the spider, a symbol of resistance who is able to evade the oppressor through cunning and trickery. In Native American mythology, it is coyote, a cultural hero with the magical power of transformation. In Indian religion, it is Krishna, the divine prankster who's trickery has a moral purpose.

The *kinesthete* is the player who engages play through the body. The kinesthete focuses on movement, not winning. Pushing the body and feeling the outcome is the goal. The kinesthete needs to move in order to think.

The *explorer* engages play through exploration and the imagination. On a physical level, the explorer likes new places. On an emotional one, the explorer pursues new feelings or the deepening of feelings. Relationally, the explorer likes meeting new people. Intellectually, new subjects and points of view are welcome.

The *competitor* likes competitive games and plays to win. Competitors prefer clear goals and keeping score, whether the game is solitary or social. Competitors are easy to spot in social groups because they enjoy high status.

The *director* likes to be in charge. Planning, coordinating, and organizing is the director's idea of fun because they enjoy directing other people. They are dynamic and often the epicenter of social groups.

The *collector* wants to have the most, the best, and the most interesting objects and experiences. Arranging and systematizing is the form of play. Collectors may go to great lengths in efforts to collect. They may collect in a solitary manner or with other collectors with similar obsessions.

The *artist/creator* enjoys making things. This includes arts and crafts, inventing, constructing, designing, and decorating. Artist/creators are sensitive to shape, color, and texture. The goal is to make something new, fix something, or make something look great.

Finally, the *storyteller* uses imagination to create new worlds. Storytellers enjoy imagining, perfecting reality through playful enhancements. They invite others into their world. Writing, reading, performing are all examples of storytelling play. Because the imagination is always available, this type of play is available in almost any situation. In contrast to the competitor, the storyteller enjoys a good match.

Most people are a mix of play personalities. Identifying one's play personality can lead to greater self-awareness and provide clarity about the most effective ways to interact with others. Since one's play personalities are typically formed in childhood, thinking back to how one played as a child is a good start in identifying one's play personality.

Though play is often considered extraneous to everyday life, except perhaps in the lives of children, play researchers have come to see it as critical to evolution. In fact, play is viewed as part of a general theory of human relationships. Human relationships are about engaging otherness. Therefore, a general theory of human behavior is a way of understanding of how humans engage difference. These **modes of engagements are pathways for experience**, that is, recognized trajectories that help us understand what to expect from events. There are at least four: work, play, communitas, and ritual.

Humans use work to accomplish objectives outside of the work event. One may enjoy one's work; however, the main focus is the product or end result. Play, in contrast, focuses on process. Players seek position through balancing privilege and engagement; that is, they seek advantage while trying to stay engaged with the other. In both work and play, people assert their will.

In contrast, in communitas and ritual, people surrender to external direction. Communitas are public experiences, such as carnivals or musical concerts, in which people wander seeking satisfying experiences. Rituals, however, have clear goals. Their focus is transformation from one state to another.

To be human is to be in relationship. To be in relationship is to be aware of one's standing vis-à-vis others. Issues of status are part of this awareness. Play is one of the four ways that humans make sense of engagement experiences, or interactions, which are a key structure for experiences in the world.

KEY MODES OF EXPERIENCE		
Mode	Will	Focus
Work	Assert	Accomplish objectives
Play		Process of balancing of privilege and engagement
Communitas	Surrender	Satisfying experiences
Ritual		Transformation from one state to another

Interactions are attempts by self and others to impose strategies of action. In interactions, one seeks to impose one's will on the others while trying to balance two seemingly contradictory desires: stimulation and security. The desire for stimulation leads one to seek challenging relationships, while the desire for security seeks stability.

Human interactions are an alternation of claims, a series of claims and counterclaims. One has preferences in interactions with others, or interaction patterns — recognizable trajectories that help preserve and direct energy. These are four trajectories called patterns of self-location: privilege, subordination, marginality, and engagement.

Simply put, *privilege* is the possession of special rights, the advantageous position in relationship to valued resources. The valued resources are wealth, power, prestige, and knowledge. Privilege is an imbalance of rights and responsibilities, between claims and counterclaims. A privileged person can make demands of others without reprisal. They have certain immunities that allow them to walk through the world relatively unhindered by the demands of others. They are masters at securing compliance. Ultimately, privileged people are able to make their own meaning and impose meaning on the world more than they are required to accept the meaning making of others. They set the terms of the interaction. This self-location is valued and extolled in Western societies.

Subordination is the position of being the object of obligations, to be constrained at every turn. Most people want to be in charge of their own destiny. Specifically, they want to choose the standards by which they evaluate their own lives. However, people also need boundaries within which to live their lives and clarity on how to proceed. These boundaries and procedures may be self-defined or defined by others. In the subordinate location, meaning making is imposed by others. One accepts the directives of others. Further, one may understand oneself in the terms of the other. In Western society, this location is not valued and is seen as one to be escaped.

Marginality is separation from others. Marginalized people do not impose their will — or meaning making — on others; nor do others impose their will on them. However, the marginal person continues to orient toward the society. The marginalized are on the margins of reality, not apart. The benefit of this location is the pleasure that comes from escaping the will of others. The downside is that the marginalized are not able to influence the society through engagement in meaning making. Marginality can be forced on a person or group of people or can be chosen. When it is forced, as with minoritarian groups or outsiders, this location is not valued. Outsiders are viewed as people who wish to belong to a group that will not have them. When it is chosen, as with the rebel who seeks to remake society, the location is valued. Rebels look at the society critically and have enough relative separation to engage in creative alternatives. However, they may not have the societal resources to fully realize their alternative visions.

Finally, *engagement* is the location of being fully engaged in interactions with others. To be human is to balance self and other, to coordinate obligations to others. This is how people articulate themselves. Engagement is the give and take of both influencing others and being influenced by others. In interactions, one is often confronted with demands that are external and challenging, that is, the meaning making, will, and claims of others. To be engaged is to participate in challenges that one deems worthy. The roles are active. One places claims on others, and others place claims on oneself. The pattern is a balance of assertion and compliance, rights and responsibilities, freedom and dependence. This location of reciprocity is the most productive for human relationships. It promotes the experience of joy, defined as expanding the self through meeting others.

Though play is one of the modes of experience, it is ultimately a way of being in the world, a state that encourages one to play god. In the ancient Vedic scriptures, which aim for self-realization, the fulfillment of one's possibilities, play is the modality of the gods. While Shiva is the elemental, unformed power, Sakti is the manifestation of that power, formed power — *lila* is the creative play that manifests the world. Thus, one can bring a playful approach to the other modes of experience.

KEY PATTERNS OF SELF LOCATION			
Location	Definition	Advantage	Disadvantage
Privilege	The possession of special rights	Can make demands of others without reprisal	
		Is not subject to the demands of others	
Subordination	To be the object of obligations	Clear boundaries	Constrained by the directives of others
			Understands the self in terms of the other
Marginality	Separation from others	Escape the challenge of others	Inability to influence society
Engagement	Being fully engaged in reciprocal interactions with others	Promotes growth and joy	
		The most productive for location for human relationships	

Questions for Consideration for Living in Play Mode

1.   What brought you joy as a child?

2.   With which play personalities do you identify?

3.   What are your self-location patterns?

The Structure of Games
Ordering Interactions

12

P lay that features clear rules is called games. Games are a key structure of play. They are ordered forms of play, microcosms, or little worlds, with established and clear rules of engagement. Games have three main aspects: the *choice* to play, under clear *rules*, for a *period of time*. The concept of games can be applied to any activity that has these three aspects.

There are two main kinds of games, big games and little games. Big games have impact beyond the game event to the society at large. They have economic, political, and social implications. These games challenge cultural norms, such as the activities of artists and comedians who, through their work, modify current expectations. They disrupt the rules of discourse to make room for others and modify the standard, the rules of the game at the societal level. Little games have impact only within the game event. Here the focus for players is on being judged by the same standards used to judge other players, or fairness.

Games also contain the two conditions of flow states (see chapter 8, Supreme Choice) — working at the limits of the self toward a meaningful goal with adequate feedback loops, and the ability to focus one's attention to detect relevant patterns, or the matching of new data with information retrieved from memory.

Games order (and reorder) one's interactions with others. Order is a condition of prescribed arrangement among component parts that is perceived or imposed as standard for proper functioning. Order provides clarity about how an experience will unfold and the various roles in it. These roles include understanding of what one can ask of others and what others can ask. This is status — one's position in relation to others.

People of high status are those allowed to command and control others. Thus, they typically like order. High-status people tend to enjoy games that emphasize good form and sportsmanship and seek games that reflect the advantages they have. Low-status people, those subject to the command and control of others, use games as an opportunity to experience the pleasure of high status that they do not currently have in social interactions. They are not loyal to order; instead they seek to disorder social standards. They understand that norms are social, that is, created and sustained in interactions with others. Unwilling to accept the terms of current conditions for interaction, they seek to break the rules of discourse. However, there is a balance to strike. If they go too far in challenging social norms, they will not be understood by others; but if they do not go far enough, their effort falls flat. It fails to grab attention. The disruption must be interesting or pleasurable. Thus, **high-status people tend to idealize reality in their play, and low-status people seek to realize their ideals through play.**

Games order reality on three levels: cultural, social, and psychological. The *cultural level* is the space of public meaning systems. These are shared patterns that make one's behavior comprehensible, or understandable, to others. They direct thoughts, feelings, and actions that allow one to behave properly and respond effectively to the actions of others. They provide standards of truth, beauty, justice, and utility. The cultural level concerns itself with the rule of form, both symbolic and material. These public meaning systems are further specialized by gender, race and ethnicity, class, age, sexual orientation, and religious orientation — which form subcultures. At the cultural level, play is orderly to the extent that players conform to the current cultural rules and is disorderly to the extent that players ignore, reject, or modify the rules. There are two factors to pay attention to at this level: the extent to which the game is named and institutionalized and to which it is rule bound or spontaneous. For example, if one were to look at the Black Lives Matter movement of the United States as a game, one could say that it was named but not institutionalized and that it seeks to be both rule bound and spontaneous. In 2013, the Black Lives Matter moniker became known throughout the United States and beyond in response to the acquittal of Trayvon Martin's accused murderer, George Zimmerman. The movement sought to structure itself for large-scale social change, while resisting institutionalization. It sought to support distributed, or network, leadership and was reluctant to name itself in the terms of philanthropic foundations for financial support, that is, as an organization. It sought to provide guiding principles and policy platforms to guide more spontaneous and distributed action, balancing rule boundedness and spontaneity. As a movement, it began to protest police brutality against black bodies and ultimately focused on the liberation of black people in a white-dominant culture. The Black Lives Matter movement is a subculture seeking to disrupt, or disorder and reorder, cultural institutions that effectively dominate black people.

The *social level* focuses on the rules of interaction patterns, or the nature of personal relationships in game performances. These focus on expected behavior regarding the balance of wills, or alternating claims. The first factor at this level is the extent to which the game is competitive or cooperative. There are four possible interaction patterns along these lines. In directly competitive games, the player blocks the actions of others as they compete for the same goal. These are zero-sum games, such as boxing, Monopoly, and card games. Indirectly competitive games feature parallel player activity toward the same goal, as in bingo and businesses that sell different products that serve the same needs. In directly cooperative games, players respond to the actions of others in a supportive manner that integrates goals, such as in board games like Community, online multiplayer games like Minecraft, and group dancing like ballet and line dancing. These games support participation over competition. Finally, in indirectly cooperative games, the players' individual actions support a common goal, as in quilting bees or a research consortium.

THE INTERACTION PATTERNS OF GAMES

Directly Competitive	Player blocks the actions of others toward the same goal

Indirectly Competitive	Parallel play activity toward the same goal
Directly Cooperative	Player responds supportively to the actions of others in a way that integrates goals
Indirectly Cooperative	Individual player actions support a common goal

The second factor at the social level is the extent to which the players accept the terms of the games: the rules, beliefs, and roles. Social events such as a marriage, a theater performance, and a day at work are examples of games with such recognized terms. One understands what is expected. Order is found in players' acceptance of the terms. The third factor is the extent to which meaning is determined externally, where authorities decide the nature of one's challenges or the standards by which one is measured. Ideally, one is able to choose the challenges one accepts and negotiate the standards by which one measures action. However, order at the social level is found to the extent that one accepts external meaning. Thus, a balance here is also sought.

At the *psychological level*, games order cognitive schema: mental models that help one make sense of the world, conceptual frameworks for making sense of experiences. That can be as simple as dog or bird, or as complex as roles and prejudice. They help one integrate current reality for use in future reality. There are four factors in considering psychological levels of order. The highest is activity control, the extent to which the player controls the type of activity and the rules. Direction control is the extent to which the player influences the direction and character of the action; action control is the extent to which the player is able to take a turn in controlling the action, that is the pace and sequence of the activity. When the player is able to choose when to enter and exit the activity, the player has participation control. This is the lowest form of psychological control. Order is found at the psychological level to the extent that the player controls the activity, the direction it takes, the moves that can be made, and when to enter and exit the game.

PSYCHOLOGICAL POINTS OF CONTROL IN GAMES

High	Activity Control	Player controls activity type and rules
	Direction Control	Player influences direction and character of the action, which controls how others participate
	Action Control	Player takes turn in controlling the action, or activity pace and sequence
Low	Participation Control	Player ability to choose when to enter and leave the activity

Games are the play event that illuminates the space between order and disorder. The concept of order is not power neutral. It is the current balance of power.

Players seek advantage, whether individually or collectively, and they aim to order this advantage. Players also want to be challenged and to challenge, which brings disorder. Ultimately, players seek to strike a balance between boredom, which comes from excessive control, and anxiety, which comes from too little control. Players push the boundaries of consciousness and capacity to live as freely as possible in any given moment.

FORMS OF ORDER			
Level	**Definition**	**Key Issues**	**Order/Disorder**
Cultural	Shared patterns of behavior — or public meaning systems — that direct thoughts, feelings, and actions	The extent to which the game is named and institutionalized	Order is found when the players conform to the rules
		The extent to which the game is rule bound, or spontaneous	Disorder is found when the players ignore, reject, or modify the rules

FORMS OF ORDER			
Level	Definition	Key Issues	Order/Disorder
Social	Interaction patterns, or nature of personal relationships in games	The extent to which the game is competitive or cooperative	Cooperation is more orderly than competition
		The extent to which players accept the terms of the game	Order is found in player acceptance of the terms
		The extent to which players accept external meaning making and standards	Order is found in player acceptance of external meaning making and standards
Psychological	Conceptual frameworks for making meaning of experiences	Activity control	Order is found when player controls activity type and rules
		Direction control	Order is found when player controls action direction and character
		Action control	Order is found when players take turn controlling pace and sequence
		Participation control	Order is found when players choose activity entry and exit

Looking more closely at the structural elements of games offers key aspects to consider in designing or outlining a game. Here we consider ten that cover the bases, though not all games contain each element. These are the elements to be understood by all players and that may be contested.

The *purpose* of the game is the goal, the end result the players aim to achieve. In chess, it is to checkmate one's opponent. In Rummy, it is to get the highest number of points through creating high-value spreads, with rounds ending when the first player runs out of cards. In a spelling bee, it is to be the last one to not misspell a word.

The *procedure for action* is the method, or the specific actions taken to reach the goal. In some board games, players move pieces around the board according to the dice roll. In tag games, players run to avoid being tagged by other players and being "it," the tagger. In a business meeting, it is the agenda.

The *rules governing action* are the principles of the game that direct player conduct. They are standards of behavior. In the game Giant Steps, the player must move backwards if the magic phrase "Mother may I?" is not spoken when making a request for movement. In musical chairs, the player who is left without a chair when the music stops must exit the game.

The *number of participants* states participation restrictions, any limits on the minimum or maximum number of players that must be observed in order for the game to function effectively. Hide-and-go-seek requires at least two players. Football is very specific, requiring two teams, each with 11 players. A hockey game requires 12 players at a time, 6 for each team. Bingo supports any number of players.

The *roles of participants* outline the different functions and status, or power positions. Power may be shared or differentiated. In hockey, there are different roles, or differentiated power positions: three forwards, two defense, and one goalie on each team. Business meetings also have roles: facilitators, decision makers, note takers, and participants. In backgammon, neither player has more role power.

The *payoff* in a game is the values assigned to the different possible outcomes. In blackjack, it's money. In spin the bottle, it's a kiss. In a relay race, it's a medal. In a business meeting, it's shared understanding or agreements.

The *required abilities* are the capacities players must have to play the game effectively. These may be cognitive, such as memory and evaluation; sensory motor, or bodily movement and endurance; or affective, such as alert calmness and identification. In card games, players benefit from being able to remember the cards played and from which suits. The five basic skills of basketball are dribbling, shooting, running, passing, and jumping.

Interaction patterns are the different possible player relationships. There are at least eight. Intraindividual games take place within the player's mind and body and require no contact with external people or objects. Examples are meditation and finger flexion tricks. In extraindividual games, a player directs action toward an object in the environment, such as in solitaire and jigsaw puzzles. Aggregate games are those in which multiple players direct their actions toward objects in the environment, such as bingo and roulette. In interindividual games, players direct their action toward each other in a competitive way, as in checkers, tennis, and paintball. Unilateral games have three or more players, with one being the antagonist, or "it," as in tag and dodgeball. Multilateral games occur between three or more players who direct competitive action toward each other but have no particular antagonist, as in Scrabble or poker. Intragroup games are cooperative games with two or more players working toward a mutual goal, such as cat's cradle, silent line up, and group juggle. Finally, intergroup games are competitive action between two or more intragroups, as in soccer, basketball, and mock trial.

PLAYER INTERACTION PATTERNS

Intraindividual	Within single player's mind and body
Extraindividual Action	The player directs action toward an object in the environment

Aggregate	Multiple players direct action toward objects in the environment
Interindividual	One player directs competitive action toward another player
Unilateral	Three or more players with one of the players as the antagonist, or "it," directing action toward the other players
Multilateral	Three or more players directing competitive action toward each other with no particular antagonist
Intragroup	Cooperative games with two or more players working together toward a mutual goal
Intergroup	Competitive action between two or more intragroups

Environmental requirements are the physical settings necessary for a game. Squash requires a four-walled court. Water polo requires a pool. Ice hockey requires an ice rink. Charades requires no particular environment.

Finally, *required equipment* is the objects used in the course of the actions of a game. Badminton requires rackets, a bird, and a net. Basketball requires a court, two hoops, and a basketball. Twenty questions requires no objects.

THE STRUCTURAL ELEMENTS OF GAMES

Purpose	The goal
Procedure for Action	Specific actions toward goal
Rules Governing Action	Principles that direct player behavior
Number of Participants	Any minimum of maximum limit on players
Roles of Participants	The different functions and statuses, or power positions
Payoff outcomes	The values assigned to the different possible
Required Abilities	The capacities players need to play the game effectively

Interaction Patterns	The different possible player relationships
Environmental Requirements	The physical setting necessary for a game
Required Equipment	The objects used in the course of the actions of a game

The structural elements of games are helpful in understanding the many factors to consider in ordered interactions with others. Status and power relationships are woven through games. Games help players fine-tune capacities and regulate affect for mastery. In fact, research shows that games change how people respond to stress, challenges, and pain. Games allow players to develop physical, mental, emotional, and social resilience. A gameful mindset is an advantage in life — to seek out otherness, to intentionally engage in claims and counterclaims, to refine oneself at one's learning edge.

The Party Game

Sign Reading

13

Purpose

The Goal

The Party game comes from the field of theater. Actors play it to learn the subtle differences in status between characters — how they manifest and are transformed. The purpose of this game is to see the signs of patterns of domination. In terms of the three main patterns of resistance — sign reading, deconstruction, and reconstruction — this is a sign reading game. See chapter 2, Interaction Patterns.

Procedure for Action

Specific Actions Toward Goal

The facilitator explains the game by reviewing the purpose and procedure for action up to number 8. The rest are enacted in sequence:

1. The facilitator chooses the host of the party.

2. The facilitator hands out one card to each person, except the host.

3. Each player, except the host, is now playing a partygoer role and holds the card facing out on their forehead, ensuring not to see the card.

4. The card represents the player's status in the game; Ace is the lowest, King is the highest.

5. The host stands by an imaginary door and greets each partygoer upon entering, based on the status indicated by the card at their forehead.

6. After being greeted by the host, partygoers enter an imaginary party room.

7. Partygoers interact with others according to the status indicated by the card on their forehead, all the time ensuring not to see their own card.

8. Partygoers attempt to determine their own status based on how others are interacting with them.

9. The facilitator observes throughout, reminding players of the rules, as needed, and looking for the moment when it appears that all players have a sense of their status. This may take about 10 minutes.

10. The facilitator asks players to line up in accordance to what they think is their status, still without looking at their card.

11. When players agree on the ordering, the facilitator asks them to look at their cards and check to see if they did indeed line up according to status.

12. The facilitator asks the players what they noticed and learned about status from the interactions.

Here are more detailed debrief questions:

- What were the most local/immediate power relations?
- What narrative makes this power relationship possible?
- How is this power relationship linked to other power relationships to form a strategy of dominance?
- How was the power relationship modified in the interaction?

Rules Governing Action
Principles That Direct Player Behavior

1. Players should be careful not to see their own card.

2. Players should ascertain their own status only according to interactions.

3. Players should note the details of an interaction that carry status.

Number of Participants
Any Minimum or Maximum Limit on Players

This game requires at least four (4) people and can be played with up to about 10 to 12.

Roles of Participants

The Different Functions and Statuses, or Power Positions

The *facilitator* explains the game and procedure for action. The facilitator also chooses the host, gives out the cards to the partygoers, launches the game, oversees the game, and facilitates the debrief.

The *host* stands at an imaginary door greeting the other players as they cross the threshold into an imaginary party.

The *players* seek to interact with each other according to status in an effort to ascertain their own status.

Payoff

The Values Assigned to the Different Possible Outcomes

The payoff is that the players learn to identify the signs of status in interactions. In a cohesive group, the payoff may also be that players know how to talk about status explicitly, which may lead to more clarity about, and alignment on, expressed values and behavior.

Required Abilities

The capacities players need to play the game effectively

1. Players need to be able to move around.

2. Players need to be willing to interact in an intentional way for about 10 to 15 minutes.

3. Players need to be able to reflect on and attempt to articulate their experience.

4. The facilitator needs to be able to, unobtrusively, gain and direct the attention of the players toward the goal, according to their roles, in accordance to the rules.

5. The facilitator needs to be able to facilitate a debrief discussion among the players about the game, what they experienced, noticed, and learned; and close the game in a manner that honors the potential vulnerabilities of the players.

Interaction Patterns

The Different Possible Player Relationships

In terms of the four personal interaction patterns of games, or the degree to which the game is competitive or cooperative, this is both a directly competitive and directly cooperative game. See chapter 12, The Structure of Games. The player blocks the actions of the other players toward the same goal, that is, their own status, while at the same time slotting into their status vis-à-vis the other players, or partygoers.

In terms of the eight player interaction patterns, or possible player relationships, this is a multilateral game. See chapter 12. It focuses on three or more players who direct competitive action toward each other. There is also an aspect of intragroup patterns, as players also form subgroups with people they perceive as being part of a key similar group. At a high level, high-status people will seek to interact with other high-status people.

More specifically, while this game has an overall pattern made up of Ace to King, there are variable options for how the partygoers, and even the host, decide to interact "according to status." For example, the partygoers may play out an interaction in which a lower-status person accepts the higher status of another because it is seen as earned or legitimate. Or a lower status does not accept the higher status of another and seeks to overturn the dynamic. Does it work? What forces support or block this attempted shift? It could also be that a higher-status person tries to hide her dominant status.

Environmental Requirements

The Physical Setting Necessary for a Game

This game can be played indoors or outdoors.

Required Equipment

The Objects Used in the Course of the Actions of a Game

This game requires a regular deck of cards.

The Stand, Sit, Kneel Game
Deconstruction

14

Purpose
The Goal

The Stand, Sit, Kneel game is from the field of theater. Actors play it to learn how to amplify the status differences in scenes and reflect shifts in status.

The purpose of this game is to understand the relationships between the signs of patterns of domination. In terms of the three main patterns of resistance — sign reading, deconstruction, and reconstruction — this is a deconstruction game. See chapter 2, Interaction Patterns.

Procedure for Action
Specific Actions Toward Goal

The facilitator explains the game by reviewing the purpose and procedure for action.

1. The facilitator invites three (3) players to play the actors and the rest to be the audience.

2. The audience proposes a setting in which the actors act out an improvisational scene, such as a place. The setting should be something that is already in motion and supports the development of a clear storyline. For example, New Year's in a bar, just after the ball has dropped. Or the playground after a kid has just fallen off the slide.

3. Usually, it's good to let the actors decide their relationships and situations themselves, based on the setting. If they have a really good setting, they should be able to create a scene. However, if the actors need it, or if the audience wants to be more specific, the audience can also provide a situation. For example, New Year's in a bar, just

after the ball has dropped, and you and your friends are reflecting on the past year. Or the playground after a kid has just fallen off the slide, and the parents, who are from different socioeconomic groups, are trying to figure out what happened and how to interact with each other across differences.

4.   The actors begin to interact and move around as they improvise a scene. They must immediately move into a position, based on the plot, where there is one person standing, one person sitting, and one kneeling.

5.   The actors each have an objective they are pursuing (something they are trying to get from the others), and every line reflects that, though at all times one person should be standing, one person sitting, and one person kneeling.

6.   Any shift in position should be prompted by a change in the plot.

7.   If the facilitator feels that the actors have gotten too comfortable in one position for too long, the facilitator can say "switch," and the actors must change position, still in relationship to the plot.

8.   A scene may run between 5 and 10 minutes.

9.   The facilitator begins the debrief by asking the actors what they noticed and learned about status from the interactions.

Here are more detailed debrief questions for all participants.

• What were the most local/immediate power relations?

• What narrative makes this power relationship possible?

• How is this power relationship linked to other power relationships to form a strategy of dominance?

• How was the power relationship modified in the interaction?

Rules Governing Action
Principles That Direct Player Behavior

1.   The actors are improvising a setting, always ensuring that one is standing, one sitting, and one kneeling.

2.   Any shift in position must be prompted by a change in the plot.

Number of Participants

Any Minimum or Maximum Limit on Players

This game should have at least seven (7) players and can have as many as can fit in the room and hear the actors "on stage."

Roles of Participants

The Different Functions and Statuses, or Power Positions

The *facilitator* helps divide players into actors and audience and facilitates the game and debrief.

Three (3) players agree to play *actors*.

The rest of the players play the *audience*.

Payoff

The Values Assigned to the Different Possible Outcomes

Players usually find that their change in position represents a change in status, as follows:

- Standing tends to be high status. For example, it may represent someone who is directing the action, staying out of the mayhem, or rising above everything.
- Sitting tends to be fairly high status. For example, it may represent someone who is trying to figure something out before taking action.
- Kneeling is almost always low status. For example, being a child or someone scrubbing the floor.

Required Abilities

The Capacities Players Need to Play the Game Effectively

1. Players need to be able to move around.
2. Players need to be willing to interact in an intentional way for about 10 to 15 minutes.
3. Players need to be able to reflect on and attempt to articulate their experience.
4. The facilitator needs to be able to, unobtrusively, gain and direct the attention of the players toward the goal, according to their roles, in accordance with the rules.

5.   The facilitator needs to be able to facilitate a debrief discussion among the players about the game — what they experienced, noticed, and learned — and close the game in manner that honors the potential vulnerabilities of the players.

Interaction Patterns
The Different Possible Player Relationships

In terms of the four personal interaction patterns of games, or the degree to which the game is competitive or cooperative, this is a directly competitive game. See chapter 12, The Structure of Games. The player blocks the actions of the other players toward the same goal, that is, their particular status at the moment. However, overall, the goal is to increase status vis-à-vis the other actors.

In terms of the eight player interaction patterns, or possible player relationships, this is a multilateral game. See chapter 12. It focuses on three players who direct competitive action toward each other while acknowledging status differentials and slotting to the most appropriate position.

More specifically, while this game has an overall pattern made up of three people alternating between three levels of status — reflected physically by them standing, sitting, or kneeling — there are variable options for how the actors decide to interact "according to status." For example, the actors may play out an interaction in which a lower status person accepts the higher status of another because it is seen as earned or legitimate. Or a lower status does not accept the higher status of another and seeks to overturn the dynamic. Does it work? What forces support or block this attempted shift? It could also be that a higher-status person tries to hide dominant status.

Environmental Requirements
The Physical Setting Necessary for a Game
This game requires a room.

Required Equipment
The Objects Used in the Course of the Actions of a Game
This game requires one chair.

The Tongue Twister Game

Reconstruction

15

Purpose

The Goal

The Tongue Twister game is from the field of theater. Actors play it to learn how to be in tune with their stage partner.

The purpose of this game is to use the signs of interactions to tell a different, more mutual, story. In terms of the three main patterns of resistance — sign reading, deconstruction, and reconstruction — this is a reconstruction game. See chapter 2, Interaction Patterns. In this game, two people practice being in sync.

Procedure for Action

Specific Actions Toward Goal

1. The facilitator explains the game by reviewing the purpose and procedure for action.
2. Players are divided into groups of two (2).
3. Players sit across each other in their team, facing each other.
4. The facilitator gives each team a tongue twister to practice.
5. When the players are ready, the facilitator goes around the room as the teams each say their tongue twister for the rest as best they can. (See Rules Governing Action below.)
6. The facilitator decides which team performed the best.

Here are more detailed debrief questions:

- What were the most local/immediate power relations?
- What narrative makes this power relationship possible?
- How is this power relationship linked to other power relationships to form a strategy of mutuality, or egalitarian relationships?

• How was the power relationship modified in the interaction?

Rules Governing Action
Principles That Direct Player Behavior

1.   Players repeat the tongue twister as fast as possible.

2.   Players repeat the tongue twister with the best diction possible.

3.   Players repeat the tongue twister as in sync with the partner as possible.

4.   Players keep repeating the tongue twister as long as possible without making a mistake.

Number of Participants
Any Minimum or Maximum Limit on Players

This game can be played with as few as two (2) players, in which case the goal is not to be the best among partner teams but to beat your best time.

Roles of Participants
The Different Functions and Statuses, or Power Positions

The *facilitator* explains the game and procedure for action. The facilitator also launches the game, oversees the game, and facilitates the debrief.

The *players* seek to perform in sync with their partner.

Payoff
The Values Assigned to the Different Possible Outcomes

The payoff is that the players become more in sync and can perform in unified purpose.

Required Abilities
The Capacities Players Need to Play the Game Effectively

1.   Players need to be willing to interact in an intentional way for about 3 to 5 minutes.

2.   Players need to be able to reflect on and attempt to articulate their experience.

3.   The facilitator needs to be able to, unobtrusively, gain and direct the attention of the players toward the goal, in accordance to the rules.

4.   The facilitator needs to be able to facilitate a debrief discussion among the players about the game, what they experienced, noticed, and learned; and close the game in manner that honors the potential vulnerabilities of the players.

Interaction Patterns
The Different Possible Player Relationships

In terms of the four personal interaction patterns of games, or the degree to which the game is competitive or cooperative, this is a directly cooperative game. See chapter 12, The Structure of Games. The players must respond supportively to the actions of others in a way that integrates goals. The goal is alignment.

In terms of the eight player interaction patterns, or possible player relationships, this is an intragroup game where two or more players work together toward a mutual goal. See chapter 12.

Environmental Requirements
The Physical Setting Necessary for a Game

This game can be played indoors or outdoors.

Required Equipment
The Objects Used in the Course of the Actions of a Game

Traditional tongue twisters are used in this game, such as these samples.

EASY

- I thought, I thought of thinking of thanking you.
- Three thin thinkers thinking thick thoughtful thoughts.
- She sells seashells by the seashore.
- Round the rough and rugged rock the ragged rascal rudely ran.
- Six sleek swans swam swiftly southwards.
- A big black bug bit a big black dog on his big black nose!

CHALLENGING

- I wish to wish the wish you wish to wish, but if you wish the wish the witch wishes, I won't wish the wish you wish to wish.

- If practice makes perfect and perfect needs practice, I'm perfectly practiced and practically perfect.

- I saw Susie sitting in a shoeshine shop. Where she sits she shines, and where she shines she sits.

- Why do you cry, Willy? Why do you cry? Why, Willy? Why, Willy? Why, Willy? Why?

- The big black bug bit the big black bear, but the big black bear bit the big black bug back!

- Love's a feeling you feel when you feel you're going to feel the feeling you've never felt before.

DIFFICULT

- Whether the weather be fine, or whether the weather be not, whether the weather be cold, or whether the weather be hot, we'll weather the weather, whether we like it or not.

- Betty bought a bit of butter. But the butter Betty bought was bitter. So Betty bought a better butter, and it was better than the butter Betty bought before.

- A fly and flea flew into a flue. Said the fly to the flea, "What shall we do?" "Let us fly," said the flea. Said the fly, "Shall we flee?" So they flew through a flaw in the flue.

- A twister of twists once twisted a twist, and the twist that he twisted was a three-twisted twist. Now in twisting this twist, if a twist should untwist, would the twist that untwisted untwist the twists?

- A tree toad loved a she-toad who lived up in a tree. He was a two-toed tree toad, but a three-toed toad was she. The two-toed tree toad tried to win the three-toed she-toad's heart, for the two-toed tree toad loved the ground that the three-toed tree toad trod. But the two-toed tree toad tried in vain. He couldn't please her whim. From her tree toad bower, with her three-toed power, the she-toad vetoed him.

- This is a story about four people named Everybody, Somebody, Anybody, and Nobody. There was an important job to be done, and Everybody was sure that Somebody would do it. Anybody could have done it, but Nobody did it. Somebody got angry about that, because it was Everybody's job. Everybody thought Anybody could do it, but Nobody realized that Everybody wouldn't do it. It ended up that Everybody blamed Somebody, when Nobody did what Anybody could have done.

The Meisner Game
Reconstruction

16

Purpose
The Goal

The Meisner game is from the field of theater. Actors play it to learn how to be in tune with their stage partner. Sanford Meisner, an American theater master, developed a unique approach to acting focused on an actor's instinctive response to the surrounding environment, rather than "in the head" or intellectual approaches. In his approach, repetition is key for moving beyond filters to underlying emotions.

The purpose of this game is to use the signs of interactions to tell a different, more mutual, story. In terms of the three main patterns of resistance — sign reading, deconstruction, and reconstruction — this is a reconstruction game. See chapter 2, Interaction Patterns. In this game, two people practice being in sync.

It is particularly useful when the stakes are high, as with people who work together, especially if there is a presenting challenge. The goal is to get beyond filters, to what is at the heart of the challenge. This game could end badly because one player's honesty may hurt the other. The facilitator should watch for this and stop the partners before they get to that point, although the facilitator may not succeed. Proceed if interested in unfiltered engagement.

Procedure for Action
Specific Actions Toward Goal

1. The facilitator explains the game by reviewing the purpose and procedure for action.

2. Players are divided into groups of two (2).

3.   Partners sit facing each other.

4.   One partner begins by stating something about the other partner, for example, "Your shirt is red."

5.   The second partner repeats what was said, but in the first person, for example, "My shirt is red."

6.   The partners repeat the same statmements until one notices something different and changes the statement, for example, "I think you think I'm wrong about..."

7.   When the time feels right (perhaps after about 3 to 5 minutes), the partners may switch, and the second partner starts a new round, repeating procedures 4 to 6.

Here are debrief questions:

• What were the most local/immediate power relations?
• What narrative makes this power relationship possible?
• How is this power relationship linked to other power relationships to form a strategy of mutuality, or egalitarian relationships?
• How was the power relationship modified in the interaction?

Rules Governing Action
Principles That Direct Player Behavior

Players should state observations in increasing intimacy, from statements about general physical observations to statements about perceived thoughts, to statements about perceived feelings, balancing honesty with gentleness.

Number of Participants
Any Minimum or Maximum Limit on Players

This game is played in groups of two (2) players, with a minimum of one group.

Roles of Participants
The Different Functions and Statuses, or Power Positions

The *facilitator* explains the game and procedures for action. The facilitator also launches the game, oversees the game, and facilitates the debrief.

The *players* seek to check perceptions about the other partner and gain insight into the physical, intellectual, and emotional state of the partner.

Payoff

The Values Assigned to the Different Possible Outcomes

The payoff is that the partners explore each other's question to gain understanding, and aiming to cut through filters.

Required Abilities

The Capacities Players Need to Play the Game Effectively

1. Players need to be willing to interact in an intentional way for about 6 to 10 minutes.

2. Players need to be able to reflect on and attempt to articulate their experience.

3. The facilitator needs to be able to, unobtrusively, gain and direct the attention of the players toward the goal, in accordance to the rules.

4. The facilitator needs to be able to facilitate a debrief discussion among the players about the game — what they experienced, noticed, and learned — and close the game in manner that honors the potential vulnerabilities of the players.

Interaction Patterns

The Different Possible Player Relationships

In terms of the four personal interaction patterns of games, or the degree to which the game is competitive or cooperative, this is a directly cooperative game. See chapter 12, The Structure of Games. The players must respond supportively to the actions of others in a way that integrates goals.

In terms of the eight player interaction patterns, or possible player relationships — this is an intragroup game where two or more players work together toward a mutual goal. See chapter 12.

Environmental Requirements

The Physical Setting Necessary for a Game

This game can be played indoors or outdoors.

Required Equipment

The Objects Used in the Course of the Actions of a Game

There are no objects used in this game.

The Yes, But/Yes, And Game

Sign Reading, Deconstruction

17

Purpose

The Goal

The Yes, But/Yes, And game comes from the field of theater. As highlighted in chapter 10, Theater as Interaction and Identity Creation, most interactions break down into either blocking or accepting, where the proposed action of the other is either circumvented or integrated into one's own. Blocking can be either a form of control or a way of seeking safety. High-status people are more likely to block than lower-status people, though some may do so to protect themselves from the actions of high-status people.

However, to engage in mutual relationship, one must move toward acceptance in interactions. In improvisational theater, as in everyday life, moments are made up of offers and acceptances. The mutual making and acceptance of offers creates a generative cycle, and in theater it keeps the story moving.

In improvisational theater, the actor should be able to respond in the moment appropriately and seamlessly to another actor's words, speaking tone, and body language. The goal for the actor is to keep the story going, even in tricky interactions. Therefore, blocking and accepting are key acting skills.

The purpose of this game is to understand the relationships between the signs of patterns of domination. In terms of the three main patterns of resistance — sign reading, deconstruction, and reconstruction — this is a sign reading and deconstruction game. See chapter 2, Interaction Patterns. This game helps players understand, through experience, the power of resistance and acceptance, or seeing the signs of domination and exploring the different response choices.

Procedure for Action

Specific Actions Toward Goal

1. The facilitator explains the game by reviewing the purpose and procedure for action.

2. Players are divided into groups of two (2).

3. Players decide which will be dominant and which subordinate in their team.

4. The dominant player begins the interaction with a request. For example, "Morton, will you get me a glass of wine?"

5. The subordinate player always responds by explaining that fulfilling the request is not possible. For example, "Yes, but that won't be possible. We're all out of wine."

6. This goes on back and forth, with the subordinate player tying in the dominant player's every request until it culminates in a disaster.

7. Then, the dominant player makes an opening statement. For example, "What a hot and miserable day!"

8. The subordinate player responds by building on the dominant player's statement. For example, "Yes, and it would be great to go to a pool."

9. This goes on back and forth, with the subordinate player always adding to the dominant player's statement until it reaches a high note.

Here are debrief questions:

- How did you feel about the different experiences of resistance and acceptance?
- What are the differences between resistance and acceptance?
- How was the power relationship modified in the interaction?
- Did you recognize certain situations from your life in these two experiences?

Rules Governing Action

Principles That Direct Player Behavior

1. Players must be disciplined about resisting or building, blocking or accepting.

Number of Participants
Any Minimum or Maximum Limit on Players

This game is played in groups of two (2) players, with a minimum of one group.

Roles of Participants
The Different Functions and Statuses, or Power Positions

The *facilitator* explains the game and procedure for action. The facilitator also launches the game, oversees the game, and facilitates the debrief.

The *players* seek to perform in sync with their partner.

Payoff
The Values Assigned to the Different Possible Outcomes

The payoff is an understanding of how power works in both resistance and acceptance.

Required Abilities
The Capacities Players Need to Play the Game Effectively

1. Players need to be willing to interact in an intentional way for about 6 to 10 minutes.
2. Players need to be able to reflect on and attempt to articulate their experience.
3. The facilitator needs to be able to, unobtrusively, gain and direct the attention of the players toward the goal, in accordance to the rules.
4. The facilitator needs to be able to facilitate a debrief discussion among the players about the game — what they experienced, noticed, and learned — and close the game in manner that honors the potential vulnerabilities of the players.

Interaction Patterns
The Different Possible Player Relationships

In terms of the four personal interaction patterns of games, or the degree to which the game is competitive or cooperative, this is a directly competitive (Yes, But) and directly cooperative (Yes, And) game. See chapter 12, The Structure of Games.

In terms of the eight player interaction patterns, or possible player relationships — this is an interindividual game and intragroup game. See chapter 12. When the players are blocking, there is a competition between two individuals, but when they are cooperating, they are working together toward a mutual goal.

Environmental Requirements
The Physical Setting Necessary for a Game

The game can be played indoors or outdoors.

Required Equipment
The Objects Used in the Course of the Actions of a Game

There are no objects used in this game.

The Circle Game
Reconstruction

18

Purpose
The Goal

The Circle game is from the field of theater. Actors play it to learn how to be in tune with the other actors on stage. When on stage, even if the actor is not directly interacting with another actor, the actor should always be in tune with those sharing the scene.

The purpose of this game is to use the signs of interactions to tell a different, more mutual, story. In terms of the three main patterns of resistance — sign reading, deconstruction, and reconstruction — this is a reconstruction game. See chapter 2, Interaction Patterns. In this game, a group of people becomes an ensemble. Players learn to work together by sensing each other, without having to look at each other. This is a very challenging exercise that only works sometimes.

Though all games help people work together better, there are specific games, like ensemble games, of which this is one, in which the goal is not to win but to achieve group cohesiveness. If a group cannot do it, it means it is not aligned; the members are not in sync with each other. They must either continue playing the game until they achieve alignment or find the cause of the block. Being unable to do this is worse than losing; it is failing. All it takes is one person who insists on leading.

Procedure for Action
Specific Actions Toward Goal

1. The facilitator explains the game by reviewing the purpose and procedure for action.

2.   The facilitator invites players to stand in a large circle.

3.   As a group, without using any words, making eye contact, or using physical communication, players must decide to run into the circle at the same time that everyone else does to create a smaller circle.

4.   The group pauses in the smaller circle.

5.   Then, again, as a group, without using any words, making eye contact, or using physical communication, players must decide collectively to run back out at the same time to form the larger circle.

6.   This continues for 3 to 5 minutes.

7.   The facilitator observes and lets the group know if it is falling into a rhythm, which would mean players are not sensing each other but falling into a rhythm. For example, remembering that last time they waited about 5 seconds to run into the circle, they wait 5 seconds this time.

8.   The facilitator points out infractions kindly. For example, "Sofia, remember not to lead," or "Krishna, remember not to make eye contact," or "Group, remember that you want to stay out of a set rhythm as much as possible."

9.   The facilitator asks players what they noticed and learned about moving as a group.

Here are more detailed debrief questions:

• What were the most local/immediate power relations?

• What narrative makes this power relationship possible?

• How is this power relationship linked to other power relationships to form a strategy of mutuality, or egalitarian relationships?

• How was the power relationship modified in the interaction?

Rules Governing Action
Principles That Direct Player Behavior

1.   No one player should be cuing the group to follow the player in or out of the circle.

2. Players can look around, but they are not supposed to make any signals with their eyes, or fall into a rhythm; that is cheating.

Number of Participants
Any Minimum or Maximum Limit on Players

This game requires at least six (6) people. The more, the better.

Roles of Participants
The Different Functions and Statuses, or Power Positions

The *facilitator* explains the game and procedure for action. The facilitator also launches the game, oversees the game, and facilitates the debrief.

The *players* seek to sense each other indirectly in order to anticipate the group's next step, so that they may flow with it, contracting and expanding as a group.

Payoff
The Values Assigned to the Different Possible Outcomes

The payoff is that the group becomes more aligned and in sync. Players learn to subconsciously tune in to each other's movements. The ensemble can move as one. It has one unified purpose.

Required Abilities
The Capacities Players Need to Play the Game Effectively

1. Players need to be able to move around.
2. Players need to be willing to interact in an intentional way for about 3 to 5 minutes.
3. Players need to be able to reflect on and attempt to articulate their experience.
4. The facilitator needs to be able to, unobtrusively, gain and direct the attention of the players toward the goal, in accordance to the rules.
5. The facilitator needs to be able to facilitate a debrief discussion among the players about the game — what they experienced, noticed, and learned — and close the game in manner that honors the potential vulnerabilities of the players.

Interaction Patterns

The Different Possible Player Relationships

In terms of the four personal interaction patterns of games, or the degree to which the game is competitive or cooperative, this is a directly cooperative game. See chapter 12, The Structure of Games. The players must respond supportively to the actions of others in a way that integrates goals. The goal is alignment.

In terms of the eight player interaction patterns, or possible player relationships, this is an intragroup game where many players work together toward a mutual goal. See chapter 12.

Environmental Requirements

The Physical Setting Necessary for a Game

This game can be played indoors or outdoors.

Required Equipment

The Objects Used in the Course of the Actions of a Game

There are no objects used in this game.

The Lane Game

Reconstruction

19

Purpose
The Goal

The Lane game is from the field of theater. Actors play it to learn how to be in tune with the other actors on stage. When on stage, even if the actor is not directly interacting with another actor, the actor should always be in tune with others sharing the scene.

The purpose of this game is to use the signs of interactions to tell a different, more mutual, story. In terms of the three main patterns of resistance — sign reading, deconstruction, and reconstruction — this is a reconstruction game. See chapter 2, Interaction Patterns. In this game, a group of people becomes an ensemble. Players learn to work together by sensing each other, without having to look at each other. This is a very challenging exercise that only works sometimes.

Though all games help people work together better, there are specific games, like ensemble games, of which this is one, in which the goal is not to win but to achieve group cohesiveness. If a group cannot do it, it means it is not aligned; the members are not in sync with each other. They must either continue playing the game until they achieve alignment or find the cause of the block. Being unable to do this is worse than losing; it is failing. All it takes is one person who insists on leading.

Procedure for Action
Specific Actions Toward Goal

1. The facilitator explains the game by reviewing the purpose and procedure for action.

2.   To warm up, the facilitator invites players to walk around the room without focusing on anything in particular, seeing the rest of the room out of their peripheral vision and the other senses.

3.   Still warming up, the players may try to follow another player without looking but by paying attention with the other senses and tracking the other player with concentration around the room. This helps the player figure out how to be aware of other people without directly looking at them.

4.   The players stand in a straight line, side by side, with about 2 to 4 feet between each person, like swimming lanes. The facilitator may make the lanes clear by placing chairs at the end of each lane.

5.   The facilitator asks the players to do actions that increase in complexity, which the players all attempt to do at the same time, for example, "Walk," "Run," "Sit, "Jump," "Stand." Players should walk along their lane, cuing their movement off the movements of the other players without looking them. The players are sensing and hearing when other players are jumping or standing and reacting with them.

6.   This continues for 3 to 5 minutes.

7.   The facilitator points out infractions kindly, for example, "Maya, remember not to lead," or "Taylor, remember not to make eye contact."

8.   The facilitator asks players what they noticed and learned about moving as a group.

Here are more detailed debrief questions:

- What were the most local/immediate power relations?
- What narrative makes this power relationship possible?
- How is this power relationship linked to other power relationships to form a strategy of mutuality, or egalitarian relationships?
- How was the power relationship modified in the interaction?

Rules Governing Action
Principles That Direct Player Behavior

1.   No one player should be cuing the others.

2. Players can look around, but they are not supposed to make any signals with their eyes or fall into a rhythm either; that is cheating.

Number of Participants
Any Minimum or Maximum Limit on Players

This game requires at least four (4) people.

Roles of Participants
The Different Functions and Statuses, or Power Positions

The *facilitator* explains the game and procedure for action. The facilitator also launches the game, oversees the game, and facilitates the debrief.

The *players* seek to sense each other indirectly in order to anticipate the group's next step, so that they may flow with it, contracting and expanding as a group.

Payoff
The Values Assigned to the Different Possible Outcomes

The payoff is that the group becomes more aligned and in sync. Players learn to subconsciously tune in to each other's movements. The ensemble can move as one. It has one unified purpose.

Required Abilities
The Capacities Players Need to Play the Game Effectively

1. Players need to be able to move around.

2. Players need to be willing to interact in an intentional way for about 3 to 5 minutes.

3. Players need to be able to reflect on and attempt to articulate their experience.

4. The facilitator needs to be able to, unobtrusively, gain and direct the attention of the players toward the goal, in accordance to the rules.

5. The facilitator needs to be able to facilitate a debrief discussion among the players about the game — what they experienced, noticed, and learned — and close the game in manner that honors the potential vulnerabilities of the players.

Interaction Patterns

The Different Possible Player Relationships

In terms of the four personal interaction patterns of games, or the degree to which the game is competitive or cooperative, this is a directly cooperative game. See chapter 12, The Structure of Games. The players must respond supportively to the actions of others in a way that integrates goals. The goal is alignment.

In terms of the eight player interaction patterns, or possible player relationships, this is an intragroup game where many players work together toward a mutual goal. See chapter 12.

Environmental Requirements

The Physical Setting Necessary for a Game

This game can be played indoors or outdoors.

Required Equipment

The Objects Used in the Course of the Actions of a Game

There are no objects used in this game. However, chairs may be placed at the end of each lane to guide the players.

The Body Language Game

Sign Reading

20

Purpose

The Goal

The Body Language game comes from the field of theater. Actors play it to learn the subtle differences in status between characters — how they manifest and are transformed.

The purpose of this game is to see the signs of patterns of domination. In terms of the three main patterns of resistance — sign reading, deconstruction, and reconstruction — this is a sign reading game. See chapter 2, Interaction Patterns.

Procedure for Action

Specific Actions Toward Goal

1. The facilitator explains the game by reviewing the purpose and procedure for action.

2. The facilitator divides the players into two groups, one dominant and one subordinate.

3. The facilitator reviews the key body language that connotes status. See below.

4. For 1 to 3 minutes, as long as the players can sustain it, the dominant players walk around the room enacting dominant body language, and the subordinate players walk around in a subordinate manner.

Here are debrief questions:

- What were the most local/immediate power relations?
- What narrative makes this power relationship possible?

- How is this power relationship linked to other power relationships to form a strategy of dominance?
- How was the power relationship modified in the interaction?

Rules Governing Action

Principles That Direct Player Behavior

1.   Players should be disciplined about staying in the assigned status.

2.   Players should note the behavior of other players.

3.   Players should note their own feelings and thoughts as they play out their status.

STATUS AND BODY LANGUAGE		
Area	HI Status Dominant	LO Status Subordinate
Eye Contact	Staring	Looking away
	Looking away,	looking back
Posturing	Hold head still while talking	Move head while talking
	Expose belly	Protect belly
	Legs spread apart	Toes pointing inwards
	Relaxed	Anxious
Movements	Smooth	Jerky
	Hands away from face while talking	Hands near face while talking
	Slow	Fast
Space	Belongs to them	Cedes to others
	Flow into others	Avoid flowing into others

Number of Participants

Any Minimum or Maximum Limit on Players

This game requires at least four (4) people. The more, the better.

Roles of Participants

The Different Functions and Statuses, or Power Positions

The *facilitator* oversees the game.

The *players* seek to stay in their assigned status and interact with each other according to status.

Payoff

The Values Assigned to the Different Possible Outcomes

The payoff is that the players learn to identify the signs of status in interactions. In a cohesive group, the payoff may also be that players know how to talk about status explicitly, which may lead to more clarity about and alignment on expressed values and behavior.

Required Abilities

The Capacities Players Need to Play the Game Effectively

1.   Players need to be able to move around.

2.   Players need to be willing to interact in an intentional way for about 1 to 3 minutes.

3.   Players need to be able to reflect on and attempt to articulate their experience.

4.   The facilitator needs to be able to, unobtrusively, gain and direct the attention of the players toward the goal, according to their roles, in accordance to the rules.

5.   The facilitator needs to be able to facilitate a debrief discussion among the players about the game — what they experienced, noticed, and learned — and close the game in manner that honors the potential vulnerabilities of the players.

Interaction Patterns

The Different Possible Player Relationships

In terms of the four personal interaction patterns of games, or the degree to which the game is competitive or cooperative, this is a directly competitive or directly cooperative game depending on which status the player is playing and how the player mitigates status. See chapter 12, The Structure of Games.

In terms of the eight player interaction patterns, or possible player relationships, this is a multilateral game. See chapter 12. It focuses on three or more players who direct competitive or cooperative action toward each other. There is also an aspect of intragroup patterns, as players also form subgroups with people they perceive as being part of a key similar group. At a high level, high-status people will seek to interact with other high-status people.

Environmental Requirements

The Physical Setting Necessary for a Game

The game can be played indoors or outdoors.

Required Equipment

The Objects Used in the Course of the Actions of a Game

There are no objects used in this game.

The Switching Game

Reconstruction

21

Purpose

The Goal

The Switching game is from the field of theater. Actors play it to learn how to be in tune with their stage partner and use action to drive status.

The purpose of this game is to use the signs of interactions to tell a different, more mutual, story. In terms of the three main patterns of resistance — sign reading, deconstruction, and reconstruction — this is a reconstruction game. See chapter 2, Interaction Patterns. In this game, two people practice playing out a status and then switching it, to learn fluency in status switching and status sharing.

What makes *Waiting for Godot* a good play for understanding status is that the lines are nonsense, so it is very easy to play high or low status with any lines. With a more defined play, some lines are high status and some are low.

The play has two main characters, Vladmir and Estragon, who are longtime friends. Vladimir acts as if he thinks he is superior to Estragon, and Estragon continuously rejects the subordinate status Vladimir offers him to play.

Procedure for Action

Specific Actions Toward Goal

1. The facilitator explains the game by reviewing the purpose and procedure for action.
2. Players are divided into groups of two (2).
3. Each group receives a short scene from *Waiting for Godot* (about one and a half to two pages).

4.   Players decide which will be dominant and which subordinate.

5.   Players practice their lines for 5 to 10 minutes.

6.   Players read or say, if memorized, their lines to each other while they play out their status. Players may also memorize the main exchange points and say them in their own words, or in improvisational style.

7.   When the facilitator calls out "Switch!" the player playing high status switches to low status and the low status player finds a way to switch to high status.

8.   Players read or say the lines in the new status.

9.   This can go on for one round of alternating status, or two or three.

Here are debrief questions:

· What were the most local/immediate power relations?

· What narrative makes this power relationship possible?

· How is this power relationship linked to other power relationships to form a strategy of mutuality, or egalitarian relationships?

· How was the power relationship modified in the interaction?

Rules Governing Action
Principles That Direct Player Behavior

1.   Players must be disciplined about acting out their status while delivering nonsense dialogue.

2.   Players must be vigilant about finding openings for switching status when it is called.

Number of Participants
Any Minimum or Maximum Limit on Players

This game is played in groups of two (2) players, with a minimum of one group.

Roles of Participants
The Different Functions and Statuses, or Power Positions

The *facilitator* explains the game and procedure for action. The facilitator also launches the game, oversees the game, and facilitates the debrief.

The *players* seek to perform in sync with their partner according to status and switch status when it is called.

Payoff
The Values Assigned to the Different Possible Outcomes

The payoff is understanding how to consciously and intentionally flow through status sharing and shifting.

Required Abilities
The Capacities Players Need to Play the Game Effectively

1. Players need to be able to read, and ideally memorize, a few lines in a play.

2. Players need to be willing to interact in an intentional way for about 3 to 5 minutes.

3. Players need to be able to reflect on and attempt to articulate their experience.

4. The facilitator needs to be able to, unobtrusively, gain and direct the attention of the players toward the goal, in accordance to the rules.

5. The facilitator needs to be able to facilitate a debrief discussion among the players about the game — what they experienced, noticed, and learned — and close the game in manner that honors the potential vulnerabilities of the players.

Interaction Patterns
The Different Possible Player Relationships

In terms of the four personal interaction patterns of games, or the degree to which the game is competitive or cooperative, this is a directly cooperative and directly competitive game, depending on whether one is agreeing to the status one is playing or trying to flip it. See chapter 12, The Structure of Games.

In terms of the eight player interaction patterns, or possible player relationships, this is an intragroup game where two or more players work together toward a mutual goal. See chapter 12.

Environmental Requirements

The Physical Setting Necessary for a Game

The game can be played indoors or outdoors.

Required Equipment

The Objects Used in the Course of the Actions of a Game

Short, 1½ to 2 page excerpts from *Waiting for Godot* are used in this game. The facilitator may provide the book for players to choose excerpts or provide them, such as the following.

Waiting for Godot

Act I

A country road. A tree. Evening.

Estragon, sitting on a low mound, is trying to take off his boot. He pulls at it with both hands, panting. He gives up, rests, tries again. As before.
Enter Vladimir.

Estragon:	[*giving up again*]: Nothing to be done.
Vladimir:	[*advancing with short, stiff strides, legs wide apart*] I'm beginning to come around to that opinion. All my life I've tried to put from me, saying, Vladimir, be reasonable, you haven't yet tried everything. And I resume the struggle. [*He broods, musing on the struggle. Turning to Estragon.*] So there you are again.
Estragon:	Am I?
Vladimir:	I'm glad to see you back. I thought you were gone forever.
Estragon:	Me too.
Vladimir:	Together again at last! We'll have to celebrate this. But how. [*He reflects.*] Get up till I embrace you.
Estragon:	[*irritably*] Not now, not now.
Vladimir:	[*hurt, coldly*] May one inquire where His Highness spent the night?
Estragon:	In a ditch.
Vladimir:	[*admiringly*] A ditch! Where?

Estragon:	[*without gesture*] Over there.
Vladimir:	And they didn't beat you?
Estragon:	Beat me? Certainly they beat me.
Vladimir:	The same lot as usual?
Estragon:	The same? I don't know.
Vladimir:	When I think of it ... all these years ... but for me ... where would you be ... [*Decisively.*] You'd be nothing more than a little heap of bones at the present minute, no doubt about it.
Estragon:	And what of it?

Waiting for Godot

Act I

A country road. A tree. Evening.

Estragon:	Charming spot. [*He turns, advances to front, halts facing auditorium.*] Inspiring prospects. [*He turns to Vladimir.*] Let's go.
Vladimir:	We can't.
Estragon:	Why not?
Vladimir:	We're waiting for Godot.
Estragon:	[*despairingly*] Ah! [*Pause.*] You're sure it was here?
Vladimir:	What?
Estragon:	That we were to wait.
Vladimir:	He said by the tree. [*They look at the tree.*] Do you see any others?
Estragon:	What is it?
Vladimir:	I don't know. A willow.
Estragon:	Where are the leaves?
Vladimir:	It must be dead.
Estragon:	No more weeping.
Vladimir:	Or perhaps it's not the season.
Estragon:	Looks to me more like a bush.

Vladimir: A shrub.

Estragon: A bush.

Vladimir: A—. What are you insinuating? That we've come to the wrong place?

Estragon: He should be here.

Vladimir: He didn't say for sure he'd come

Estragon: And if he doesn't come?

Vladimir: We'll come back tomorrow.

Estragon: And then the day after tomorrow.

Vladimir: Possibly.

Estragon: And so on.

Vladimir: The point is—

Estragon: Until he comes.

Waiting for Godot

Act I

A country road. A tree. Evening.

Vladimir: [*Estragon sits down on the mound. Vladimir paces agitatedly to and fro, halting from time to time to gaze into the distance off. Estragon falls asleep. Vladimir halts finally before Estragon.*] Gogo!... Gogo!... GOGO! [*Estragon wakes with a start.*]

Estragon: [*restored to the horror of his situation*] I was asleep! [*Despairingly.*] Why will you never let me sleep?

Vladimir: I felt lonely.

Estragon: I had a dream.

Vladimir: Don't tell me!

Estragon: I dreamt that—

Vladimir: DON'T TELL ME!

Estragon: [*gesture toward the universe*] This one is enough for you? [*Silence.*] It's not nice of you Didi. Who am I to tell my private nightmares to if I can't tell them to you?

Vladimir: Let them remain private. You know I can't bear that.

Estragon: [*coldly*] There are times when I wonder if it wouldn't be
            better for us to part.

Vladimir: You wouldn't go far.

Estragon: That would be too bad, really too bad. [*Pause.*] Wouldn't it,
            Didi, be really too bad? [*Pause.*] And the goodness of the
            wayfarers. [*Pause. Wheedling.*] Wouldn't it, Didi?

Vladimir: Calm yourself.

Estragon: [*voluptuously*] Calm ... calm ...

Waiting for Godot

Act II

Next day. Same time.

Same place. [A country road. A tree. Evening.]

Estragon: What a day!

Vladimir: Who beat you? Tell me.

Estragon: Another day done with.

Vladimir: Not yet.

Estragon: For me it's over and done with, no matter what happens.
            [*Silence.*] I heard you singing.

Vladimir: That's right, I remember.

Estragon: That finished me. I said to myself, He's all alone, he thinks I'm
            gone forever, and he sings.

Vladimir: One is not master of one's moods. All day I've felt in great
            form. [*Pause.*] I didn't get up in the night, not once!

Estragon: [*sadly*] You see, you piss better when I'm not there.

Vladimir: I missed you ... and at the same time I was happy. Isn't that a
            queer thing?

Estragon: [*shocked*] Happy?

Vladimir: Perhaps it's not quite the right word.

Estragon: And now?

Vladimir: Now?... [*Joyous.*] There you are again.... [*Indifferent.*] There
            we are again.... [*Gloomy.*] There I am again.

Estragon: You see, you feel worse when I'm with you. I feel better alone too.

Vladimir: [*vexed*] Then why do you always come crawling back?

Estragon: I don't know.

Vladimir: No, but I do. It's because you don't know how to defend yourself. I wouldn't have let them beat you.

The Status Master Game
Sign Reading, Deconstruction, Reconstruction

22

Purpose
The Goal

The Status Master game was designed to explore the seven patterns of domination — tolerance, objectification, assimilation, authority, objectivity, accumulation, and certainty. See chapter 2, Interaction Patterns.

The purpose of this game is to understand how the core dominant interaction patterns show up in interactions and increase the player's choices for action. This game engages all of the three main patterns of resistance: sign reading, deconstruction, and reconstruction. See chapter 2.

Procedure for Action
Specific Actions Toward Goal

VARIATION 1

1. The facilitator explains the game by reviewing the purpose and procedure for action.

2. Players are divided into groups of two (2).

3. Each group decides on an interaction scene from their experience that can be understood as an example of one of the seven dominant patterns.

4. The groups write out the first three to four interactions, about a page, making it a prompt for an improvisational scene between two (2) people.

5. Each group plays out their scene and improvises different endings that increase their choices for responses, with a goal of liberation or egalitarian interaction.

Here are debrief questions:

- What were the most local/immediate power relations?
- What narrative makes this power relationship possible?
- How is this power relationship linked to other power relationships to form a strategy of mutuality, or egalitarian relationships?
- How was the power relationship modified in the interaction?

VARIATION 2

1. The facilitator explains the game by reviewing the purpose and procedure for action.

2. The facilitator invites two (2) players to be actors "on stage" to improvise dominant pattern interaction scenes.

3. The rest of the players are the audience. The audience proposes prompts to the actors. The facilitator clarifies prompts, checks for agreement on proposed prompt with the actors, and launches scenes (and ends them if the need arises).

4. The actors play out a version of the scene.

Here are debrief questions:

- What were the most local/immediate power relations?
- What narrative makes this power relationship possible?
- How is this power relationship linked to other power relationships to form a strategy of mutuality, or egalitarian relationships?
- How was the power relationship modified in the interaction?

The debrief may lead to proposals for different endings that increase choices for responses, with a goal of liberation or egalitarian interaction, and the actors (the same or a different pair) may act out a new scene. This process may repeat many times, as the players dig deeper into the dynamics of power at play.

VARIATION 3

1. The facilitator explains the game by reviewing the purpose and procedure for action.

2. The facilitator invites two (2) players to form a team of actors "on stage" to improvise dominant pattern interaction scenes. This repeats two more times, so that there are three (3) teams.

3. The rest of the players are the audience. The audience proposes prompts to the actors. The facilitator clarifies prompts, checks for agreement on proposed prompt with the actors, and launches scenes (and ends them if the need arises, such as when the scene is boring).

4. The teams each get a chance to play out a version of the scene.

Here are debrief questions:

- What were the most local/immediate power relations?
- What narrative makes this power relationship possible?
- How is this power relationship linked to other power relationships to form a strategy of mutuality, or egalitarian relationships?
- How was the power relationship modified in the interaction?

The debrief may lead players to judge the effect of the various versions in increasing choices for responses, with a goal of liberation or egalitarian interaction.

Rules Governing Action
Principles That Direct Player Behavior

1. Players work with another player to identify a dominant pattern scene from their experience and capture it in words.

2. Players work with another player to explore the expansion of choice in the interaction.

3. Players explore the need either for finding power in an interaction, or to share power — or both.

Number of Participants
Any Minimum or Maximum Limit on Players

This game is played in groups of two (2) players. Variation 1 requires a minimum of one group. Variation 2 requires at least six (6) players, and Variation 3 at least 10. With all of the variations, the more the better.

Roles of Participants

The Different Functions and Statuses, or Power Positions

The *facilitator* oversees the game — setting it up, observing and intervening on process and procedure, and facilitating the debrief.

The *player* seeks to identify, capture, act out, and transform a dominant interaction pattern scene.

Payoff

The Values Assigned to the Different Possible Outcomes

The payoff is identifying patterns of domination and exploring response options with a goal toward expanding choice.

Required Abilities

The Capacities Players Need to Play the Game Effectively

1. Players need to be willing to interact in an intentional way for about 30 to 60 minutes, depending on the version and how deep the players go.

2. Players need to be able to reflect on and attempt to articulate their experience.

3. The facilitator needs to be able to, unobtrusively, gain and direct the attention of the players toward the goal, in accordance to the rules.

4. The facilitator needs to be able to facilitate a debrief discussion among the players about the game — what they experienced, noticed, and learned — and close the game in manner that honors the potential vulnerabilities of the players.

Interaction Patterns

The Different Possible Player Relationships

In terms of the four personal interaction patterns of games, or the degree to which the game is competitive or cooperative, this is a directly cooperative game. See chapter 12, The Structure of Games. The players must respond supportively to the actions of others in a way that integrates goals. The goal is expansion of choice. Variation 3, of course, may also be directly competitive. The players, in teams, may block the actions of the other players on different teams toward the same goal (the most powerful, possible interaction).

In terms of the eight player interaction patterns, or possible player relationships, this is an intragroup game where two or more players work together toward a mutual goal. See chapter 12, The Structure of Games.

Environmental Requirements
The Physical Setting Necessary for a Game

The game can be played indoors or outdoors.

Required Equipment
The Objects Used in the Course of the Actions of a Game

These seven domination patterns are used in this game.

TOLERANCE

One allows small doses of difference. Difference is approached as a value to the dominant; it adds nuance but does not shift power.

OBJECTIFICATION

One removes history from the interaction. One feels no personal responsibility for the past and does not see how one contributes to the condition in the present.

ASSIMILATION

One ignores difference by reducing it to sameness. If one cannot completely ignore the difference, one deems it exotic. Instead of seeking to understand a different reality, one seeks to make the other "correct" behavior.

AUTHORITY

One hides rationality. Something is because one says it is so. One does not have to justify it or provide explanations.

OBJECTIVITY

One ignores power-laden realities, believing one is taking the higher ground, claiming neutrality.

ACCUMULATION

One collects experiences and things. Quantity is made to stand in for quality. This includes deferential treatment for people of high status and dismissive treatment of a people of lower status.

CERTAINTY

One asserts one's reality as if there is no other. One knows for sure and speaks in declarative sentences. One sets the frame for the interaction, expecting the other to slide into one's narrative. It is devised to make one's reality the operative one.

The Scene Study Game

Deconstruction

23

Purpose

The Goal

The Scene Study game is from the field of theater. Actors play it to learn how to understand the interactions in a scene and the core idea driving the interactions.

The purpose of this game is to understand the relationships between the signs of patterns of domination. In terms of the three main patterns of resistance — sign reading, deconstruction, and reconstruction — this is a deconstruction game. See chapter 2, Interaction Patterns. There are five major areas to examine in exploring a scene: given circumstances, dialogue, dramatic action, characters, and idea.

Procedure for Action

Specific Actions Toward Goal

1. The facilitator explains the game by reviewing the purpose and procedure for action.

2. The player selects a scene from life to examine and answers the following questions, capturing the answers in a written, map, or image summary.

   A. What are the given circumstances of the scene?
      - Geographical location
      - Date and time
      - Economic conditions
      - Political conditions
      - Social conditions

- Previous action
- Points of views held by characters

B. What is the dialogue in the scene?

- The conversation between two or more characters in a scene, with a focus on the spoken word
- It is not just a verbal exchange but a communication of actions where each character forces his wants and needs on the other(s)
- It is always in the present tense
- Look for words, phrases, or images that capture the essences

C. What is the dramatic action in the scene?

- The clash of forces in the scene
- It is not an activity, which is the externalization of dramatic action
- The action is reciprocal — one character does something to another, and the other responds

D. Who are the characters in the scene, and what do they want?

- Examine each character's desire, will, moral stance, behavior, dress, speech — describing them with adjectives

E. What is the idea in the scene?

- Identify the core meaning of the scene

Here are debrief questions.

- What were the most local/immediate power relations?
- What narrative makes this power relationship possible?
- How is this power relationship linked to other power relationships to form a strategy of dominance?
- How was the power relationship modified in the interaction?

Rules Governing Action

Principles That Direct Player Behavior

The player(s) answer all the questions truthfully and rigorously, capturing both the analysis and the debrief.

Number of Participants
Any Minimum or Maximum Limit on Players

This game is played with at least one (1) player.

Roles of Participants
The Different Functions and Statuses, or Power Positions

The *facilitator* explains the game and procedure for action. The facilitator also launches the game, oversees the game, and facilitates the debrief. A facilitator is not necessary if there is only one player.

The *player* selects a life scene to deconstruct to understand the core idea driving the interaction.

Payoff
The Values Assigned to the Different Possible Outcomes

The payoff is understanding of the symbolic exchanges, motivations, and underlying idea in a scene.

Required Abilities
The Capacities Players Need to Play the Game Effectively

1. Players need to be willing to interact in an intentional way for about 6 to 10 minutes.

2. Players need to be able to reflect on and attempt to articulate their experience.

3. The facilitator needs to be able to, unobtrusively, gain and direct the attention of the players toward the goal, in accordance to the rules.

4. The facilitator, if available, needs to be able to facilitate a debrief discussion among the players about the game — what they experienced, noticed, and learned — and close the game in manner that honors the potential vulnerabilities of the players.

Interaction Patterns
The Different Possible Player Relationships

In terms of the four personal interaction patterns of games, or the degree to which the game is competitive or cooperative, this game does not require external interaction. See chapter 12, The Structure of Games. In terms of the eight player interaction patterns, or possible player relationships, this is an intraindividual game in which the action takes place inside the player's mind and body. See chapter 12.

Environmental Requirements

The Physical Setting Necessary for a Game

The game can be played indoors or outdoors.

Required Equipment

The Objects Used in the Course of the Actions of a Game

There are no objects used in this game.

The Character Study Game
Reconstruction

24

Purpose
The Goal

The Character Study game is from the field of theater. Actors play it to learn how to understand their character. The goal for the actor is to live truthfully under imaginary circumstances. Good acting requires holding three goals simultaneously: getting and staying in touch with the feelings in the moment, being willing to take risks, and pursuing an underlying objective using as many tactics as possible or necessary.

The purpose of this game is to understand the relationships between the signs of patterns of domination. In terms of the three main patterns of resistance—sign reading, deconstruction, and reconstruction — this is a reconstruction game. See chapter 2, Interaction Patterns. In this game, the player seeks to understand the forces driving the character, the needs and desires, as well as the obstacle(s), so that the character can effectively drive toward the objective.

Procedure for Action
Specific Actions Toward Goal

1. The facilitator explains the game by reviewing the purpose and procedure for action.

2. The player examines the self and answers the following questions, capturing the answers in a written, map, or image summary.

   A. Who is my character?

   - Occupation

   - Age

   - Status

B. What are the given circumstance of my character?

- Geographical location
- Date and time
- Economic conditions
- Political conditions
- Social conditions
- Previous action
- Point(s) of view(s) held

C. What are my character's actions?

- What is my character literally doing? For example, Stanley is yelling for Stella to come home to him.
- What is the essential action of my character? For example, begging a loved one's forgiveness.
- What is the action like to the player? For example, it's as if I broke my mother's prized family heirloom, was thrown out of the house, and to be allowed back I must beg her forgiveness.

D. What does my character want?

- The character's objectives

E. Why does my character want this?

- The character's needs

F. What is preventing my character from getting this?

- The character's obstacles

G. What is my character's relationship to other relevant characters?

H. What is my character's journey, and what are the relevant beats (a single unit of action, which changes when a new action or piece of information is introduced)?

Here are debrief questions.

- What were the most local/immediate power relations?
- What narrative makes this power relationship possible?

- How is this power relationship linked to other power relationships to form a strategy of mutuality, or egalitarian relationships?
- How was the power relationship modified in the interaction?

Rules Governing Action
Principles That Direct Player Behavior
The player(s) answers all the questions truthfully and rigorously, capturing both the analysis and the debrief.

Number of Participants
Any Minimum or Maximum Limit on Players
This game is played with at least one (1) player.

Roles of Participants
The Different Functions and Statuses, or Power Positions

The *facilitator* explains the game and procedure for action. The facilitator also launches the game, oversees the game, and facilitates the debrief. A facilitator is not necessary if there is only one player.

The *player* examines the self, seeking to understand driving forces, desires, obstacles, and options.

Payoff
The Values Assigned to the Different Possible Outcomes

The payoff is understanding one's driving forces, desires, challenges, and options.

Required Abilities
The Capacities Players Need to Play the Game Effectively

1. Players need to be willing to interact in an intentional way for about 6 to 10 minutes.
2. Players need to be able to reflect on and attempt to articulate their experience.
3. The facilitator needs to be able to, unobtrusively, gain and direct the attention of the players toward the goal, in accordance to the rules.

4.   The facilitator, if available, needs to be able to facilitate a debrief discussion among the players about the game — what they experienced, noticed, and learned — and close the game in manner that honors the potential vulnerabilities of the players.

Interaction Patterns
The Different Possible Player Relationships

In terms of the four personal interaction patterns of games, or the degree to which the game is competitive or cooperative, this game does not require external interaction. See chapter 12, The Structure of Games.

In terms of the eight player interaction patterns, or possible player relationships, this is an intraindividual game where the action takes place inside the player's mind and body. See chapter 12.

Environmental Requirements
The Physical Setting Necessary for a Game

The game can be played indoors or outdoors.

Required Equipment
The Objects Used in the Course of the Actions of a Game

There are no objects used in this game

References

Identity
Intro

Brennan, Teresa. "The Transmission of Affect in the Clinic." *The Transmission of Affect*. Ithaca, NY: Cornell University Press, 2004. 42.

Effective Interactions
Power is relational

Foucault, Michel. "Method." *History of Sexuality*, Volume 1. New York, NY: Random House, 1978.

Senge, Peter et al. "The Wedding." *Presence: Human Purpose and the Field of the Future*. Cambridge, MA: Society for Organizational Learning, 2004.

Two types of power and the central role of interactions

hooks, bell. "Changing Perspectives on Power." *Feminist Theory: From Margin to Center*. Cambridge, MA: South End Press Classics, 2000 (1984).

Foucault, Michel. "Method." *History of Sexuality*, Volume 1. New York, NY: Random House, 1978.

Interaction Patterns
Difference

Lorde, Audre. "The Master's Tools Will Never Dismantle the Master's House." *Sister Outsider*. Freedom, CA: The Crossing Press. Lorde explicitly introduces a concept that Chela Sandoval picks up later in *Methodology of the Oppressed* — a commitment to egalitarian relationships.

Patterns of domination and patterns of resistance

Sandoval, Chela. "The Rhetoric of Supremacism as Revealed by the Ethical Technology: Democratics." *Methodology of the Oppressed*. Minneapolis, MN: University of Minnesota, 2000.

Living with people who are different as the most urgent current challenge

Sennett, Richard. Inside Front Cover. *Together: The Rituals, Pleasures and Politics of Cooperation.* New Haven & London: Yale University Press, 2012.

The fetish of assertion

Sennett, Richard. "Introduction." *Together: The Rituals, Pleasures and Politics of Cooperation.* New Haven & London: Yale University Press, 2012.

Transmission of Affect

Transmission of affect

Brennan, Teresa. "The New Paradigm," "The Sealing of the Heart," "The Education of the Senses." *The Transmission of Affect.* Ithaca, NY: Cornell University Press, 2004.

Status as the main motivator

Rock, David. "Managing with the Brain in Mind." *Strategy + Business.* Autumn 2009, Issue 56. http://www.strategy-business.com/article/09306?gko=5df7f

The Sources of Power Relations

The power process, the ego psychology of Erik Erikson, the first three stages

Janeway, Elizabeth. "Origins, Births, Beginnings," "Name This Child." *Powers of the Weak.* New York, NY: Alfred A. Knopf, 1980.

Erikson, Erik H. "Growth and Crises of the Healthy Personality." *Identity and the Life Cycle.* New York, NY: WW Norton & Company, 1980 (1959).

Mind forms

Berger, Jennifer Garvey. "Key Concepts in Adult Development," "Diving Deeper." *Changing on the Job: Developing Leaders for a Complex World.* Stanford, CA: Stanford University Press, 2012.

Powerless and Powerful Identities
Hegemony and powerless identities
Forgacs, David. "Hegemony, Relations of Force, Historical Bloc." *The Gramsci Reader: Selected Writings 1916-1935*. New York, NY: New York University Press, 2000.

Baudrillard, Jean. "From Domination to Hegemony." *The Agony of Power.* Los Angeles, CA: Semiotext(e), 2010.

Supreme power and powerful identities
Singh, Jaideva. "Introduction," "Sutra 33 (of Pleasure and Pain)," "Sutra 45 (Final Achievement: Awareness of the Divine)." *Siva Sutras: the Yoga of Supreme Identity.* Delhi: Motilal Banarsidass, 1979.

Brata SenSharma, Deba. "Introduction," "Verse 9 (Liberation Practices)." *Paramarthasara of Abhinavagupta: The Essence of the Supreme Truth.* New Delhi: Muktabodha Indological Research Institute, 2007.

Choice
Intro
Foucault, Michel. "Method." *History of Sexuality*, Volume 1. New York, NY: Random House, 1978. 101.

Decision and Choice
Decision versus choice
http://dictionary.reference.com/browse/decision?s=t
http://dictionary.reference.com/browse/choice?s=t

Expected utility theory and prospect theory
Kahneman, Daniel. "Attention and Effort," "The Associative Machine," "How Judgments Happen," "Bernoulli's Errors," "Prospect Theory," "Experienced Well Being." *Thinking, Fast and Slow.* New York, NY: Farrar, Straus and Giroux, 2011.

Glucose
Pointer, Kathleen. (Reviewed by Elaine K. Luo, MD.) "Everything You Need to Know About Glucose." http://www.healthline.com/health/glucose#overview1. March 24, 2017.

The Social Aspects of Choice
Political efficacy and class

Pateman, Carole. "The sense of political efficacy and participation in the workplace." *Participation and Democratic Theory*. Cambridge, UK: Cambridge University Press, 1970.

Levels of involvement in decision making

Straus, David. "Facilitative Leadership." *How to Make Collaboration Work*. San Francisco, CA: Berrett-Koehler Publishers, 2002.

Ladder of citizen participation

Arnstein, Sherry R. "A Ladder of Citizen Participation." *Journal of the American Institute of Planners*, 1969, 35(4), 216–224.

Three faces of power

Lukes, Steven. "Power: A Radical View." *Power, A Radical View, Second Edition*. New York, NY: Palgrave Macmillan, 2005.

Minoritarian interests

Deleuze, Gilles and Felix Guattari. "November 20, 1923: Postulates of Linguistics." *A Thousand Plateaus: Capitalism and Schizophrenia*. Minneapolis, MN: University of Minnesota Press, 1987.

Supreme Choice
Control versus choice

Glasser, William. "We Need a New Psychology." *Choice Theory: A New Psychology of Personal Freedom*. New York, NY: Harper, 1998.

Flow

Csikszentmihalyi, Mihaly." "Happiness Revisited," "The Anatomy of Consciousness," "The Conditions of Flow." Flow: *The Psychology of Optimal Experience*. New York, NY: Harper Perennial Modern Classics, 2008.

Thresholds
Rites of Passage

Rites of passage, the three phases

Turner, Victor. "Liminality and Communitas." *The Ritual Process: Structure and Anti-Structure.* Piscataway, NJ: AldineTransaction, 2011 (1969).

Pollution
Douglas, Mary. *Purity and Danger: An Analysis of Concepts of Pollution and Taboo.* New York, NY: Routledge Classics Edition, 2002 (1966).

The sacred dimension
Turner, Victor. "Betwixt and Between: Liminal Period." *The Forest of Symbols: Aspects of Ndembu Ritual.* Ithaca, NY: Cornell University Press, 1967.

The social role of ritual in relieving the anxiety of difference
Sennett, Richard. "Coda." *Together: The Rituals, Pleasures and Politics of Cooperation.* New Haven & London: Yale University Press, 2012.

Rites of passage in simple and complex societies
Turner, Victor. "Liminal to Liminoid in Play, Flow, and Ritual: An Essay in Comparative Symbology." *From Ritual to Theatre: The Human Seriousness of Play.* New York, NY: PAJ Publications, 1982.

Theater as Interaction and Identity Creation
Waiting for Godot
Beckett, Samuel. *Waiting for Godot.* New York, NY: Grove Press, 1954, 22–23.

Teaching status
Keith Johnstone. "Status." *Impro: Improvisation and the Theatre.* New York, NY: Routledge/Theatre Arts Books, 1987, 41.

Social dramas
Turner, Victor. "Acting in Everyday Life and Everyday Life in Acting." *From Ritual to Theatre: The Human Seriousness of Play.* New York, NY: PAJ Publications, 1982.

Microinteractions, Theater, Status
Keith Johnstone. "Status," "Spontaneity," "Narrative Skills." *Impro: Improvisation and the Theatre.* New York, NY: Routledge/Theatre Arts Books, 1987.

Auditions, Character Creation, Intensified Interactions
Shurtleff, Michael. *Audition.* New York, NY: Bantam Book, 1978.

Theatre of the Oppressed

Boal, Augusto. *Games for Actors and Non-Actors.* New York, NY: Routledge, 2002.

Boal, Augusto. *The Rainbow of Desire.* New York, NY: Routledge, 1995.

Games
The Purpose of Play
Play as evolution

Brown, Stuart. *Play: How It Shapes the Brain, Opens the Imagination, and Invigorates the Soul.* New York, NY: The Penguin Group, 2010, 32–58.

The key features of play

Eberle, Scott G. "The Elements of Play: Toward a Philosophy and a Definition of Play." *Journal of Play*, 2014, Vol. 6, No. 2, 214–220.

Emotions

The definition is excerpted from http://medical-dictionary.thefree dictionary.com/emotional+state.

The examples are excerpted from http://www.dictionary.com/browse/ emotion?s=t

The key elements of play

Eberle, Scott G. "The Elements of Play: Toward a Philosophy and a Definition of Play." *Journal of Play*, 2014, Vol. 6, No. 2, 222–227.

Poise

The definition is excerpted from www.dictionary.com/browse/poise?s=t

Play personalities

Brown, Stuart. *Play: How It Shapes the Brain, Opens the Imagination, and Invigorates the Soul.* New York, NY: Penguin Group, 2010, 65–70.

Pathways for experience, patterns of self location

Henricks, Thomas S. "Play as a Pathway of Behavior." *Journal of Play*, 2011, Vol. 4, No. 2. http://www.journalofplay.org/sites/www.journalofplay. org/files/pdf-articles/4-2-article-henricks-play-as-a-pathway-of-behavior.pdf

The Structure of Games

Definition of game and the role of order

Henricks, Thomas S. "Orderly and Disorderly Play: A Comparison."
    Journal of Play, 2009, Vol. 2, No. 1. http://www.journalofplay.org/
    issues/2/1/article/orderly-and-disorderly-play-comparison

Definition of status

http://www.dictionary.com/browse/status?s=t.

Forms of order

Henricks, Thomas S. "Orderly and Disorderly Play: A Comparison."
    Journal of Play, 2009, Vol. 2, No. 1. http://www.journalofplay.org/
    issues/2/1/article/orderly-and-disorderly-play-comparison

The structural elements of games

Avedon, E.M. "The Structural Elements of Games." *The Study of Games.*
    Bronx, NY: Ishi Press International, 1971, 419-426.

Gameful mindset and the forms of resilience

McGonigal, Jane. *SuperBetter: The Power of Living Gamefully.* New York,
    NY: Penguin Books, 2015.

NOTE: Aside from the two game chapters noted below and *The Status
Master Game*, which I created, all games are derived from conversations
with my daughter, Saphia Suarez, who, as I mention in the introduction,
awakened my interest in acting as a skill-rich field for learning power
relations. These are all games she was taught throughout her acting
training, especially her advanced work at the Wheelock Family Theater.

The Meisner Game

Longwell, Dennis and Sydney Pollack. *Sanford Meisner on Acting.* New
    York, NY: Random House, 1987, 19–23.

The Switching Game

Beckett, Samuel. *Waiting for Godot.* New York, NY: Grove Press, 1954,
    1–2, 6, 8, 49–50.

Index

About the Author

Cyndi Suarez works with leaders in nonprofit organizations, philanthropy, social movements, and politics. She focuses on helping teams build a culture of excellence by connecting day-to-day activities with long-term vision, elegant organizational design, and meaningful participation at all levels. She specializes in network strategies—helping organizations identify their core functions and niches, and leveraging strategic partnerships to achieve large scale change. She has a passion for liberating structures.

Cyndi was executive director at Northeast Action, the first regional political strategy center in the United States. Among her consulting clients are Movement for Black Lives (Black Lives Matter national network) and United We Dream (national DREAMers network). She is currently senior editor at *Nonprofit Quarterly*, the leading nonprofit sector journal.

She has a BA in Psychology and Women's Studies from Boston College, studied Feminist Theory at the New School for Social Research, and has an MS in Community Economic Development from Southern New Hampshire University. She resides in Boston with her partner and two children.

Photo Credit:
Gwendolyn Rodriguez

A Note about the Publisher

New Society Publishers is an activist, solutions-oriented publisher focused on publishing books for a world of change. Our books offer tips, tools, and insights from leading experts in sustainable building, homesteading, climate change, environment, conscientious commerce, renewable energy, and more — positive solutions for troubled times.

We're proud to hold to the highest environmental and social standards of any publisher in North America. This is why some of our books might cost a little more. We think it's worth it!

- We print all our books in North America, never overseas
- All our books are printed on **100% post-consumer recycled paper**, processed chlorine free, with low-VOC vegetable-based inks (since 2002)
- Our corporate structure is an innovative employee shareholder agreement, so we're one-third employee-owned (since 2015)
- We're carbon-neutral (since 2006)
- We're certified as a B Corporation (since 2016)

At New Society Publishers, we care deeply about *what* we publish — but also about *how* we do business.

Download our catalogue at https://newsociety.com/Our-Catalog or for a printed copy please email info@newsocietypub.com or call 1-800-567-6772 ext 111

New Society Publishers
ENVIRONMENTAL BENEFITS STATEMENT

For every 5,000 books printed, New Society saves the following resources:[1]

25	Trees
2,259	Pounds of Solid Waste
2,485	Gallons of Water
3,242	Kilowatt Hours of Electricity
4,106	Pounds of Greenhouse Gases
18	Pounds of HAPs, VOCs, and AOX Combined
6	Cubic Yards of Landfill Space

[1]Environmental benefits are calculated based on research done by the Environmental Defense Fund and other members of the Paper Task Force who study the environmental impacts of the paper industry.

MIX
Paper from responsible sources
FSC® C016245

new society
PUBLISHERS
www.newsociety.com